Chinese Mythology

A Captivating Guide to Chinese Folklore Including Fairy Tales, Myths, and Legends from Ancient China

Free Bonus from Captivating History (Available for a Limited time)

Hi History Lovers!

Now you have a chance to join our exclusive history list so you can get your first history ebook for free as well as discounts and a potential to get more history books for free! Simply visit the link below to join.

Captivatinghistory.com/ebook

Also, make sure to follow us on:

Twitter: @Captivhistory

Facebook: Captivating History:@captivatinghistory

Contents

Introduction

Chinese mythology is a wealth of treasure composed of multiple religions, people groups, regions, and ideas. Perhaps the word *mythologies* would be more accurate than mythology, as it really encompasses so many different pantheons.

China, being a large and ancient country, also has a large and ancient tradition of mythology, legends, and folktales. Long ago, tales traveled orally and shifted in each region to be appropriate to the people's landscape, ideas, and beliefs. This means that each story or myth often has numerous versions with slightly different emphasis. In this book, these versions sometimes favor one over another and other times have been combined, but either way, this book will give you a taste of the vast realm that is Chinese mythology.

You will encounter tales of the immortals, people who have managed to contribute to or do something so special that Heaven itself decided to bless them with eternal life. In other cases, like that of the Monkey King, immortality was taken through cunning and skill. A select few, like Nüwa and the Jade Emperor, were immortals from the very beginning. Gods are also much more tangible in Chinese mythology and are even considered fallible. Even Lao Tzu, founder of Taoism, loses his perfection with the rise of Buddhism, and Buddha becomes the new infallible immortal and the exception to this rule. Though equality to the gods was attainable, and sought after, it was nothing to take for granted. Gods were highly respected and feared and many had an altar in their homes dedicated to a certain god or their ancestors.

China is an ancient and proud country for good reasons. Many of their myths, legends, and folktales are highly respected and read even today. If you are ready to be captivated by this multitude of mythologies, then snakes, spirits, demons, dragons, phoenixes, immortals, and mere mortals all await you in the pages to come.

Chapter 1 – The Origin of Earth and Humans

In the cosmic chaos, there was an egg. Inside the egg lay Pangu. He was the first god, the first giant, and simply first. Laying inside the egg, he began to form heaven and earth. Every day he would grow, and every day the heavens would rise ten feet higher and the earth would grow ten feet thicker. In the beginning, it was small and chaos still ensued all around. But each day as Pangu grew so did heaven and earth. After 18,000 years, Pangu was finally finished. Heaven was now extremely high and the earth was incredibly deep. Some say this was the formation of Yin (turbid Earth) and Yang (limpid heaven), while others would say that Yin and Yang came first, putting order into the earth and that it was only from that order Pangu first began to grow and eventually emerge.

As all things, except immortals, must die, so did also Pangu. But with his death, creation bloomed. For his body became everything we see around us. His left eye became the sun, while his right became the moon. From the strands of his beard, the stars were formed. His four limbs and five extremities became the edges of the earth and the Five Mountains. His blood formed the rivers, while his breath became the wind and clouds. His flesh turned to earth and the hairs on his head became the plants and trees to grow in it. Metals and rocks appeared from his teeth and bones, while his semen and marrow became jade and pearls. Finally, his sweat and fluids gave the earth rain so that it could hold life. Perhaps Pangu was also covered in mites and insects and it was them that became the first humans, but on that point, Nüwa would like to disagree.

The goddess Nüwa saw the earth and heaven that Pangu had formed with his dying body and his final breath. She found it so beautiful that she decided to live there. But after a while, she became lonely and decided to make people. She took up the yellow earth and began to form the people with her hands. The work was tiring and exhausted her. Eventually, she decided to grab a leather cord and simply drag it through the earth, shaking off the pieces of earth from it and creating the rest of the people that way. Now she no longer had to be alone. But after a while, the humans began to die so Nüwa started to form new people again. She knew she could not be bothered to keep forming new people constantly, so instead she gave humans a way to reproduce. After this, she withdrew, being content with what she had made. Little did she know that her work was not done yet.

Many years later, a terrible flood passed over the entire land and only two people survived, a brother and a sister. Both of them wanted to reproduce and ensure that humanity would survive, however, they felt great shame because they knew they were siblings and should not intertwine. They called to the heavens, but received no answer, so they decided to do two tests. First, they went up a high mountain, rolling down two millstones, one on each side of the mountain. Only if the stones landed next to each other could they then marry. The stones rolled down the height of the mountain, and at the bottom, both were lying next to each other. They had passed the first test and now felt comfortable getting married. Now, they went to separate locations and made fires. If the smoke from the fires intertwined with each other, they could have children and would be able to repopulate the desolate earth. After the fires had been made, both the brother and sister looked up into the sky. Slowly, the smoke that had risen separately from both their fires had become one. The brother and sister were sure they had the blessings of heaven and so they had children. However, when the sister finally gave birth, it was not the child they had expected. Instead, a spherical piece of flesh had been born. They were distraught. Had they misread the signs? For nine months they had waited for a child and instead received this abomination. They wept together, and as they wept, Nüwa heard them and appeared before them. She took a knife and cut open the spherical piece of flesh and formed not one child but many.

After humanity had been created and was reproducing, the Jade Emperor, Lord of Heaven, sent three emperors to rule over them. The first he sent was "Tian Guan," meaning ruler of heaven. He would bring them happiness, freedom, and riches. The second was "Di Guan," the ruler of earth, who would judge over the people and their actions. The third was "Shui Guan," the emperor of water, who would control the rivers and overcome diseases. These three emperors were worshipped over all of China.

When the Jade Emperor saw humans on earth and how they were living, he decided to give them some rules on food. He called to him the dung beetle and told it to tell the humans to eat once every three days. However, by the time the dung beetle had traveled back down to the humans, he had confused the message and instead told the humans to eat three times a day. The humans feasted away, gorging themselves with food, and as a result began to excrete a vast amount. At this time, Earth and Heaven were closely linked, held together by great pillars. The Jade Emperor was horrified by how revolting the humans were and could not stand the stench, so he separated Heaven and Earth to get away from the smell. To punish the beetle, he made it eat the dung that the humans excreted.

Author's Comment:

In this section, many creation myths have been fused, when often Pangu would be its own answer to the "Creation" question, and Nüwa would be another. With the creation of the humans, the brother and sister myth often does not co-exist with Nüwa, and in some versions they simply do one test and everything works out. Another version, not included here, has a giant snake give birth to all animals and then finally humans. This said, creation myths are not a dominating aspect of Chinese Mythology and there are not as many records of them as there are of other areas (like the creation of the immortals and various arts or ideas) – it seems like the origin of the human race and Earth was not as important of a question to the ancient Chinese.

The Jade Emperor is, along with Nüwa, one of the few immortals who simply exists and has no creation. Chinese mythology is filled with emperors, some which are based on real historical emperors who have been mythologized and others who simply are gods that are called 'emperors'. All of China's emperors were seen as gods, just as the Pharaohs in Egypt were. But it can be very hard to determine which emperors were gods of mythology and which were based on historical rulers. The Jade Emperor is always in Heaven and portrayed as the ruler of all the gods in Taoist mythology.

Chapter 2 – Writing and Art

Cang Jie

Huang Di, the Yellow Emperor, one of the foremost legendary rulers in ancient China, had a historiographer named Cangjie. Cangjie's role was to record everything that happened in the land. Since writing didn't exist, Cangjie used ropes of various lengths and colours to memorize every event and experience. Now, Cangjie had been born with four eyes and was incredibly gifted, but eventually even he found it difficult to remember what each piece of rope meant. He knew he had to find a new method to record history. Prostrating himself before the emperor, he asked for some time off from his duties to devise a new technique to remember everything.

Cangjie set out from the palace, meeting with people from all over the land for inspiration. He spent months following creatures, studying their shapes, signs, and patterns. After traveling across the land and studying nature and society, Cangjie finally settled down in a secluded cave, away from everything. There he began to note down symbols that reflected their character. For example, the pictograph for sun followed the sun's round shape, while the moon showed off its crescent phase. The word "field" illustrated the layering of the rice paddies. He invented a character for everything and there were as many characters as grains of rice in all of China. After Cangjie had finished his great work of inventing a written language, he set out to teach everyone. However, no one could remember all of the characters that he taught. Even Confucius himself only learned seventy percent of the original amount. When Cangjie realized that even China's most intelligent scholars could not learn all of his symbols and pictographs, he was frustrated and angry. He threw the other thirty percent away to all the other foreign countries in the world, giving them a method of writing and remembering.

When Nüwa saw the pictographs that Cangjie had created, she was angry. The character for "nü," meaning "female," an intrinsic part of Nüwa's very essence and name, had been used in numerous other characters that had negative connotations. Nüwa confronted Cangjie.

"Cangjie, do you look down on women? Thinking that our character reflects words like demon and wicked?"

Cangjie recoiled from the accusations and apologized deeply to the mother of humans. Nüwa watched and waited as he picked up his brush and set to work on a few new characters. After this, both "good" and "mother" were created with the character "nü" as a part of them.

Ma Liang and the Paintbrush

In a poor village there lived a poor boy. The boy was called Ma Liang, and he loved to draw and paint. Everywhere he went he would find a way to draw. Sometimes he would use a stick in the sand and other times he would manage to find a piece of charcoal. He became very good at drawing, so good that some said his drawings could be mistaken for real things. Despite his skill, he continued to be poor and found that his drawings could not help the other poor villagers either.

Then one night, he had a dream. An old man visited him with a beautiful paintbrush. Ma Liang had never owned a paintbrush and knew that with it he could paint marvelous things. The old man approached him and handed him the brush. "I have seen your noble heart. Use this brush to help people."

When Ma Liang woke up, the paintbrush was lying next to him. The dream had been real. But how would the paintbrush help people? Besides, he had no paint to go with it. He picked up the paintbrush and examined it. It had a beautiful mahogany handle and the brush itself was exquisitely delicate. He began to paint in the air, swishing the brush carefully as if he was painting. Suddenly, the dog that he had outlined in the air appeared and started to bark. He painted a bone on his wall, the brush adding its own colors and shadows where needed. The dog took the bone happily and ran out of Ma Liang's little hut. Ma Liang wasted no time and started to paint food, all of it becoming real.

Ma Liang headed out into the village where he knew the need was great and had heard the farmers complaining about the lack of water. He set out to the outskirts of the village and painted a river which roared to life. When the farmers heard of what he had done, they were overjoyed and thanked him. Now they could fetch water for their crops from the river. But Ma Liang knew that the crops would take time to grow and saw that many families were starving now, so he painted bowls of food for them and made sure that they could all make it to the next harvest.

After this, he set out to the next village and traveled over all of China, helping each place with what they needed.

His fame grew with his extensive travels and soon the emperor had heard of the boy with the magic paintbrush. The emperor called on Ma Liang to visit him as he wanted to personally thank Ma Liang for his services to the land.

Ma Liang knew there were still many villages to visit and lots of people who were still in need of his help, but he could not refuse the call of the emperor, so he headed to the palace and appeared before the ruler of China.

Appearing before the emperor, Ma Liang bowed low, barely having time to register the emperor's command of "Seize him!" Guards grabbed him, took his paintbrush, and threw him in prison.

The emperor was pleased to finally have the magic paintbrush in his possession. Now he could create anything he wanted. He began by drawing a large pile of gold, but nothing happened. No gold appeared. The emperor called upon his most famed artists and painters, but none of them could make anything appear out of the paintbrush. Finally, the emperor gave up, realizing that only Ma Liang would be able to wield the paintbrush. He brought the boy back to court, still in his shackles.

"If you draw for me what I ask for, I will set you free," the emperor said.

Ma Liang saw his precious paintbrush and longed to have it back. All the farmers and poor people in the land flashed through his mind. He had no desire to help a greedy emperor, but knew that without his paintbrush, he would rot in prison. "What would you like me to draw?" he asked.

"I want a mountain of gold where I can always go to get more gold."

Ma Liang was unshackled and handed the paintbrush. He began to draw, but instead of a mountain, he drew the sea.

"Why did you draw the sea? I want a mountain of gold. Not a sea." The emperor was furious and seemed tempted to throw Ma Liang back into prison.

Ma Liang quickly began to draw a mountain in the middle of the sea and filled it with enormous piles of gold. The fury in the emperor quickly subsided, replaced by a hunger shining bright in his eyes.

"Quickly!" he said. "Draw me a ship so I can collect the gold!"

Ma Liang agreed and painted the emperor a ship.

The emperor wasted no time and jumped on the ship, ordering his men to follow. As soon as they were out at sea, Ma Liang added wind and a great storm rose up. The storm became more violent as Ma Liang only added to the large waves that were brewing. They threw the ship back and forth until one huge wave crashed over it, sinking it to the bottom of the sea.

With that, the land was rid of the greedy emperor and Ma Liang set out to help the poor again. The new emperor was benevolent to Ma Liang and supported his cause, and Ma Liang and his magic paintbrush were loved by everyone in the land.

Ling Lun

Ling Lun was chosen to be the minister of music by the Jade Emperor who ordered him to invent and make music. Ling Lun thought about it and then set out to a nearby mountain. He walked around and saw many bamboo shoots. Taking one of them, he carved it into a thin pipe. He carved five holes into it and created five notes. It was a good start, and the notes were clear and different. A phoenix was flying above him, singing its beautiful song. Ling Lun's little pipe was nothing in comparison to the marvel of the phoenix song and he wanted to find a way to create similar music. He cut eleven more pieces of bamboo of various thicknesses and put them all together to make a twelve-pipe instrument. With it, he was able to catch the range of the phoenix song and make music similar to its tune.

Author's note:

The story of Ma Liang and his magic paintbrush is a popular Chinese folktale which depicts the evil of greed and the honor in helping poor people. It also shows the importance of honing your talents and using your gifts to serve others. There are many myths which depict "culture bearers," or people who contributed to creating culturally beneficial things, like Ling Lun creating the twelve-pipe instrument. Music was, and still is, highly respected in China. It was common for early Taoist scholars to study an instrument and master it as part of their learning.

Chapter 3 – Natural Disasters

The Archer Yi

The Archer

In its infancy, the earth had ten suns. Fortunately, the suns all rotated and took turns shining their light on earth, and all was well. The elder brother always started these cycles and was then followed by the rest of his siblings, each one taking his turn, before the last one finally gave way to the moon, allowing the earth to rest.

One day, the second sun decided it wanted to start shining first. Always it had been the eldest sun— why should it be so? Were they not all bright shining suns? So, the second sun joined the first and shone its light on earth. The other siblings agreed and joined in too. Suddenly, ten suns were radiating all their glory towards the earth and the earth began to suffer.

Where once trees and fields had grown, now they were all dried up. Explosions began to happen as things caught fire left and right. Very quickly, the earth was becoming a volcano, constantly ablaze, and would soon die. There was famine across the land and people were dropping dead like flies.

Yi, an archer and hunter, saw how life and nature was dying all around him and he was outraged. He grabbed his bow and the best arrows he had and headed to the tallest of mountains. After a long climb, he finally reached the top. He felt the searing heat of the tens suns incessantly shining, since the moon no longer arrived with her cool embrace. He was greeted by a god who handed him a vermilion bow and arrows with silk cords. Notching one the arrows on his new bow, Yi fired it. The arrow flew true and struck one of the suns. Instantly its light was snuffed out and it fell from the sky like a great phoenix, but never to be reborn. Yi continued, shooting down suns, until only one was left and finally balance was restored to earth. The last sun promised to only shine in its cycle and to always give way to the moon.

Reward

As thanks for his service towards mankind and earth, Yi was given an elixir of immortality. Yi took the elixir, as it would be rude to refuse, but did not consume it. He knew that if he did he would one day have to watch his wife, Chang'e, die and continue to live without her for eternity. They both agreed that they would store the elixir safely in their house but not drink it, for neither wanted to be without the other.

Yi had an apprentice named Feng Meng, who was without a doubt the second-best archer in the world, surpassed only by his master. Feng Meng realized that the only way he could be the best was to kill his master—or become immortal.

One day when Yi was out hunting monsters who had been preying on the nearby villages, Feng Meng feigned sickness and instead went to Yi's house. Feng Meng broke his way into Yi's house and searched for the elixir. When he finally entered the bedroom, he saw Chang'e with tears running down her face. In her hands was the elixir of immortality.

"Why do you do this to your master? He has trained you since you were a boy!" she said, looking at him.

"I cannot live in his shadow forever. This is the only way to surpass him," Feng Meng said, his mind set. He notched an arrow and pulled it back to his cheek. "Give me the elixir."

Chang'e looked at him sadly and tipped the bottle. Feng Meng lunged for it, not realizing it was already empty.

"As soon as I heard you sneak in, I drank it. I would rather suffer eternally than let the world suffer forever at the hand of a traitor like you." With her last words, she flew to the sky and disappeared to the moon, where she could always watch over her husband. Some of the gods were upset that she had drank the elixir as it had been meant for Yi, but they decided to give her the moon as her residence since her final act as a mortal had also been one of bravery.

When Yi finally returned home and learned what had happened, he fell to his knees and wept. Eventually he found the strength to rise and gathered all of Chang'e's favorite fruits and cakes and sacrificed them to her. The villagers who lived nearby were grateful for his heroic deeds and sympathetic to his cause, so they too sacrificed cakes to the moon. Thus, on every August 15 in the lunar calendar, people eat moon cakes to remember Yi and his beloved wife.

Feng Meng had not given up his hope of being the best. He knew he was still no match for Yi in an archery competition and couldn't become the best using any fair method. Instead he lay in wait, biding his time for Yi to come to the nearby forest. Once Yi passed by, Feng Meng struck him with a club made from a peach tree and killed him. However, Yi's fame was already secured and he became an icon and was worshipped by some as the god who diverts disasters.

Shen Nong – The First Farmer

Once upon a time, there was a man named Shen Nong. Shen Nong saw all the vast varieties of plants and trees that surrounded him, each with their own fruits and leaves. He quickly tried a few of them and realized they tasted differently. Some gave energy and were good to cook, while others were bitter or sour. He began to classify and organize them all, teaching others about which herbs or fruits were good to eat, which had healing properties, and which were poisonous. Many times, he would find a new plant, try it, and end up sick for days because of its toxic nature. However, none of this stopped him from exploring all of China and noting down the properties of all of the herbs and plants. Whenever Shen Nong found plants that were good for eating or healing, he would take them home and plant them on his farm. So, not only did Shen Nong establish the traditional Chinese healing arts, he also created the practice of agriculture. While he was farming, he realized he needed a tool to work the land and invented the plow. All the others who had started farming were soon also using the plow, which Shen Nong gladly taught them how to make and use.

One day, Shen Nong found a new plant that he had never seen before and immediately tasted it. The toxins spread through his body and he became deathly ill. Shen Nong was put in his bed and everyone knew he would soon die. Heaven looked down and saw all that Shen Nong had done for the people, how he had classified and tried all sorts of herbs and plants to help people and how he had made the plow to help the farmers. They granted him immortality. He instantly became well and continued to help people and try plants for many years before he went up to Heaven.

Taming the Rivers

In the dawn of China, the rivers ran rampant in the land, and there were many floods where people and houses were destroyed. Heaven cared not, as it believed the humans deserved it; indeed, they encouraged it. One god, Gun, who was the grandchild to the Jade Emperor, felt differently. Gun felt compassion for the humans and went down to help them. He walked along the river and started to build canals and dig ditches to lead the rivers in ways that would be beneficial to the land and the people. Gun knew the farmers already worked hard and tried to make the rivers aid them rather than hinder them.

When the other gods saw what he was doing, they were upset and smote him down. They stripped him of his immortality and killed him. However, out of his body a dragon was born. It was large, like a river, and was called Yu. The dragon saw the destruction that the rivers were still causing and flew all the way up to heaven to plead on behalf of the humans. When the ruler of heaven finally heard of the vast atrocities and realized the impact that the floods were having on the people, he finally relented and allowed Yu to get to work to ease their suffering. Heaven had also seen how hard the people were working to appease the rivers and appreciated their valiant effort. The dragon Yu raised mountains and redirected rivers to help the land and the people. He also told the people where to build canals that would allow the excess water of the river to flow out in safe ways. Through Yu and the hard work of the people, the floods ceased and the rivers were tamed.

Author's note:

There are numerous legends and myths surrounding the archer Yi—in some he is a hero, in others a villain, in some an immortal, and in other cases a human. The story that follows is a fusion of a few of these that will give you a small glimpse into his vast fame.

Shen Nong literally means "god of agriculture"; he was also very popular among botanists and physicians and often worshipped by them.

Rivers were vital to China's prosperity and were often thought to be huge, wild dragons raging in force. There are numerous myths of how the rivers were subdued and finally brought to aid the people. The archer Yi faces a river in some myths and so does the Monkey King. Historically speaking, China managed to build great ditches and dams with its vast amount of people and workforce to tame the rivers.

Chapter 4 – Li Tieguai – A Taoist Myth

Li Tieguai was a solitary man. He had withdrawn from the village life to live in a secluded cave. The busyness of village life was not for him, nor did he find the gossip appealing. Instead, he became self-sustainable and grew enough vegetables to provide for his simple meals. There was a forest nearby where he cut his own wood to make small fires and keep his mountain cave warm. The mountain also had a small stream, from which he got his water. Alongside the mountain, he had a few terraces where he grew his rice. Li Tieguai felt he had everything he needed. Each day was the same—he would work his land and then withdraw in the evening to read his Taoist scriptures. If the weather was fierce and stormy, he would spend the whole day with his scrolls.

One day as he was planting his seeds, a woodcutter appeared. Li Tieguai had never seen him before but offered him some rice and tea. The stranger talked and talked, mostly about strange things, like spirits, ghosts, and magicians. Li Tieguai listened patiently to everything.

"You are destined for great things," the stranger said. "You will be recognized as a man of wisdom and compassion and you will comfort those in need. One day, you will even be made immortal in recognition of your service."

"Wisdom is a difficult path and few can follow it—how can I ever hope to attain it? I have never pursued immortality, but I do study the Tao and I am willing to study hard."

The stranger seemed happy with Li Tieguai's response and dropped the topic. Instead, he asked, "My wisdom lacks in the ways of nature and spirits, even though I have heard many stories. I have a daughter who desires to honor me and wants me to have a long and healthy life. To do this, she wishes to study so that she can bless me in the best way. She needs a wise teacher. Will you teach her?"

Li Tieguai shook his head. "How can I do that when I myself have so much to learn?"

The stranger nodded. "You could be right." Then he left.

Three days later, the woodcutter was back. This time a beautiful girl was with him.

"This is my only daughter," the woodcutter said. "Ever since I told her of you, she has wanted nothing but to be your student. She has even stopped eating. I have had no choice but to bring her to you. Please be her teacher."

Li Tieguai looked away from the girl and back at his cave, but it was too late. The woodcutter had already disappeared with a quick remark for the girl to obey Li Tieguai in everything.

The girl approached him and knelt at his feet. Li Tieguai flushed and went back to the cave. He sat down in his corner and picked up his Taoist scriptures to study. The fire shone its light for him and kept him warm. The girl had followed him inside and started to prepare dinner for them. While it was cooking, she even cleaned the cave.

After a while, Li Tieguai felt her looking at him again.

"Master," she said. "I do not wish to disturb you in your studies. I know they are important to you. But surely you need company too. Do you not want a wife and a family to care for you when you are old?"

Li Tieguai continued to read, ignoring her.

"Please tell me your thoughts, great master. It is only the two of us here. I will not share your secrets or your doubts. You can talk to me."

He said nothing and walked to the entrance of the cave and stared outside.

"Master, I have to confess something. I did not come here to be a student, but I needed to escape my father. He had planned for me to marry an ugly man with enormous ears who walks with a limp. His whole body is twisted and hairy, unlike yours. You are a handsome man and I would love to be your wife and study with you."

Li Tieguai kept his silence and the girl continued, "I would be the best housewife you could imagine. You would want for nothing."

She kept telling him how good their life together could be as he silently stood there. Many hours passed and she even drew a picture of what their family life could look like. Finally, the night air grew cold and it was bedtime.

Li Tieguai waited until he could finally hear a steady rhythm in the girl's breathing, ensuring that she was asleep. He pulled his mattress to the corner of the cave far away from the girl and then fell asleep.

Rain poured down outside and thunder roared, startling the girl awake. She spotted Li Tieguai in his corner and snuck close to him, cuddling up beside him. Suddenly, Li Tieguai was awake and could feel the warm body of the girl next to him.

"What are you doing?" he asked, worried. "Go away, leave me."

But she only snuggled in closer, shivering. She was wearing nothing but a thin cotton dress.

"Hug me and hold me close. I'm so cold. I need your warmth."

Li Tieguai rolled further and further into the corner of the cave, growing colder as he did so. The girl kept following, whispering gently, even asking him to take her as his wife. Li Tieguai blushed again, but kept his eyes shut and tried to forget about the girl. This continued throughout the night, but Li Tieguai remained strong.

When dawn finally came, the woodcutter was back. Li Tieguai was washing his pots and had not seen the girl anywhere since last night.

"Where is my daughter?" the man asked.

"I don't know. She suddenly vanished last night."

"What did you do? Did you hurt her? Did you rape her? Why would she just vanish? What have you done?"

Li Tieguai held up his hands and shook his head. "I would never do such a thing. I have not touched your daughter nor harmed her."

The woodcutter smiled. "I know," he said. "You are a man of firm conviction and a man of honor. You have a deep understanding of Taoism and you are committed to the pursuit of it. We are similar, you and I."

Suddenly, the woodcutter transformed and became a bearded man in a long blue robe. It was Lao Zi, the immortal founder of Taoism.

"I sent the girl to tempt you and test you. You have shown true integrity and that you are not easily tricked."

Lao Zi brought out a small dumpling from his robe and gave it to Li Tieguai.

"Swallow it," he said.

Li Tieguai did as he was instructed and felt a surge of energy within him that never ceased. From then on, he was never tired, ill, thirsty, or even hungry. He began to travel the land, helping the poor and needy by defending their causes. Every few months, he would return to his cave to meditate and study the Taoist scriptures.

Li Tieguai Tempted by Treasure

Another day when Li Tieguai had been back in the cave to meditate and study his books, he took a break to study the forest. While he was walking and observing, he noticed two men. They looked nervous and secretive and were glancing around to make sure no one was looking. Li Tieguai kept himself hidden behind a tree and watched. The men had two big woven sacks and they looked heavy and full to the brim. The men searched in the tree and dug out a small alcove and stuffed the bags into it. They looked around again and, seeing no one, left the area.

Li Tieguai decided to leave too. He came back daily and noticed that the bags were still hidden. It seemed like stolen goods, but he had no idea who it had been taken from.

He went down to the village but heard nothing of anything missing. Instead, he met an old man who asked to drink tea with him. Li Tieguai, being polite, readily accepted and they sat and dined together.

"I can see that you will be a very wealthy man," the stranger said.

"You could be right," Li Tieguai responded. "I know where two bags of gold are hidden." Li Tieguai told the old man of what he had seen in the forest.

"You should take it," the man said. "It is stolen anyway. Without money you will end up bitter and unhappy. Why not go now and make sure you get the money? You can even use it to help people."

Li Tieguai shrugged off the old man's urging. "I have no need for it. I am happy with what I have."

"Your fortunes could change. A little insurance never goes amiss."

But Li Tieguai held firm. He could help people with what he had; stolen goods were not the way to earn money. Possessions were meaningless and he was content. He parted ways with the old man.

A few days later, they met again. But this time, the man's attitude had changed.

"Here, eat this," he said, holding out a dumpling for him. Li Tieguai felt he could trust the old man and did as he was told.

Immediately, he began to feel lighter as if he could float.

The man transformed before him and was now wearing long blue robes. It was Lao Zi who had come to test him again.

When Li Tieguai began to walk away, he realized he was moving much faster than before. As he walked through the town and past the temple, he was traveling faster than a swallow. Soon, he was traveling so fast that his body lifted and he soared into the air. He could fly and could now reach even more villages with his aid and counsel than before.

Li Tieguai Takes an Apprentice

Li Tieguai was now respected as a learned man and continued to help the poor and spread Taoist teachings. With his speed and flight, along with never being ill or tired, his fame had spread quickly. Eventually, Li Tieguai took on an apprentice named Li Qing. This had been at Lao Zi's request and Li Tieguai had become an official disciple of him.

One day, he was called to meet with Lao Zi again at a mountain far away.

"I must leave you," Li Tieguai said to his apprentice. "I have been summoned and must travel to Penglai Mountain.

"But that is thousands of miles away!" his student exclaimed. "It will take months to get there."

"Do not question me," Li Tieguai responded. "I will leave my body here and my soul will travel to converse with Lao Zi. If I am not back within seven days, you can burn my body, for I will have become immortal. If you study hard enough and live a life of servitude, perhaps one day you can become immortal too."

Li Tieguai then sat down and began to meditate. After a while, Li Qing saw a shimmer of smoke leave Li Tieguai's body. He put his hand in front of his master's nose and felt no breath. Being a sincere and loyal student, Li Qing did not leave his master's body for six days. However, on the morning of the seventh day, a messenger arrived.

"You must come with me," the messenger said. "Your mother is gravely ill and wants to see you before she dies."

The disciple knew it was the seventh day, so with a heavy heart, he burned his master's body and went with the messenger to see his dying mother.

On the way to his mother, not far from the cave, he met a beggar dying by the roadside. He knelt by the man to see what he could do to help and soon saw that the man was already beyond saving; there was nothing he could do. The man had short hair, ragged clothes, long eyebrows, and a disfigured leg. Next to him lay a wooden crutch, thrown to the side.

That same evening, Li Tieguai's spirit came back to look for his body. But it was nowhere to be found. He searched and searched and could not even find his disciple. Li Tieguai realized it was the seventh day and then saw the fire and the burnt ashes next to it. His body was gone. He needed to find a body fast or else he would no longer be immortal. Looking around, Li Tieguai found the deformed beggar's body that his disciple had seen earlier in the day. He knew he had no other choice and reluctantly entered the body. Just as he fit into his new form, he heard someone laugh behind him. There stood an old man with a bag of herbs and potions.

"What is so funny?" asked Li Tieguai. "Do you know me?"

"I do indeed know you. Here, take this potion. It will heal the wounds of your body and restore your health."

Li Tieguai received the potion and drank it. Immediately the vial refilled.

"This potion will never stop. With it you have the gift of healing and will be of great comfort to many people. Everyone, rich or poor, will want you to visit their home, regardless of your unfortunate looks." The old man picked up the wooden crutch next to Li Tieguai.

"This crutch shall be your aid and never falter, never rust, and never fail you." As the man spoke, the crutch changed and became iron. "From this day on, you shall join the immortals, but now I must return to Lao Zi, as I am merely his messenger."

With that, the old man started walking away down the path. But as he walked he transformed and Li Tieguai knew he had met Lao Zi again.

Li Tieguai walked the land, supported by his staff. Now he was immortal and he never ceased helping the sick and the poor.

Author's note:

Taoist mythology has a total of eight immortals of which Li Tieguai is one. His name (tie guai) actually means "iron crutch" as he was known for having a deformed leg and always walked around with his iron crutch to support himself. He is meant to have been quite ugly and perhaps the story you just read is a way of explaining why that was. But even above that, it showed that looks do not matter – what matters is helping others and seeking knowledge.

Taoists strived for knowledge and immortality and their myths show this too. Seeking immortality is the height of knowledge and the noblest thing you can do, according to Taoism.

Chapter 5 – Sun Wukong – The Monkey King

The Monkey King's Birth

In the red mountains, on top of the highest of peaks, stood a strange rock. It balanced on the edge of the mountaintop as if it would fall over at any second. For generations it had stood there, until one day, during a furious lightning storm, a lightning bolt cracked the rock open and out came a monkey. In many ways he was not like a monkey at all. He was brilliant, clever, cunning, and mischievous. But he was also faster, stronger, taller and more agile than any other monkey ever seen before.

The monkey stretched, finally awakening to life. Coming down the mountain, he found kinsmen—other monkeys—and they set out to find a home. They found a lush, beautiful mountain full of fruit and flowers. There they lived and basked in the bounties of the mountain. For a while, the monkey was happy there. The other monkeys had soon realized that he was more capable than any of them and named him king of their tribe and even of all monkeys in the world. He was now known as the Monkey King. However, eventually the Monkey King began to grow restless. Despite all the food and the good life that he lived, he realized he was still mortal and would one day die. This frustrated him and he knew he had to pursue the noblest of things—immortality. He left the mountain of fruit and flowers and found a Taoist master.

As the Taoist master's disciple, the Monkey King soon became his best student. He learned how to fly, how to clone himself and become a mirage, and he even mastered the 72 transformations, which allowed him to turn into anything he wanted. The Taoist master was so impressed with the Monkey King's talents that he renamed him Sun Wukong, meaning "Awakened to Emptiness."

Finding a Weapon

Sun Wukong was pleased with all the skills that he had picked up, but knew that he was still a mortal and that his days were numbered. He decided that he needed a weapon and armor worthy of all his skills and talent. Leaving the Taoist master, he met an old monkey who told him of the Dragon King, Ao Guang. Ao Guang's palace had thousands of weapons and he had supplied most of Heaven with their arsenal of weapons. There, the Monkey King should find a weapon worthy of his skill.

Sun Wukong flew to the Eastern Sea where he swam below the surface and looked for the palace. Eventually, at the bottom of the sea, he found a huge palace, guarded by crustaceans dressed in armor and armed with halberds and swords. Even without a weapon, Sun Wukong found them to be no match to his skills and soon entered the palace. One of the guards tried to run and warn the Dragon King of this intruder, but it was too late, as Sun Wukong was already there in the throne room.

"What is this monkey doing in my palace without an invitation? Guards! Take him away!" Ao Guang shouted, outraged at the insolence and lack of respect of Sun Wukong.

Sun Wukong merely laughed and jumped out of the way of the guards. He toyed with them, first disappearing into thin air, before reappearing and disarming them.

The Dragon King looked at Sun Wukong with new respect, but also fear. He had no desire to let a monkey destroy his palace.

"What do you want? Why do you disturb me?" The Dragon King's voice was angry and annoyed, but there was a touch of respect in it too.

"I need a weapon. As you can see, I am skilled and able, but I lack a weapon that is worthy of me. I hear you make good weapons. Give me one and I will leave you in peace."

The Dragon King fixed his eyes on the audacious monkey, and then quickly gestured to the still dazed guards and servants. "Fetch him a few weapons to try."

They scurried away and soon came back with an array of weapons.

First, a spear was brought to Sun Wukong. The guard was barely able to lift it, such was its weight. Sun Wukong spun it around as if it was a chopstick and then dropped it to the floor. "Far too flimsy," he said. The guard looked at him with new awe as he struggled to retrieve the spear.

Next came a giant sword. It was carried by several guards and the Dragon King was near certain that this would be far too heavy for the monkey.

Sun Wukong looked at the sword with his mouth agape and walked around it as if contemplating how he would pick it up. But there was a glint of mischief in his eyes and suddenly he stopped his charade and took up the sword, swishing it in the air before twirling it around on the palm of his hand.

Now the Dragon King trembled. "Bring him the heaviest weapon we have," he ordered.

Finally, out came a massive halberd carried by dozens of guards. Sun Wukong approached it and tried to pick it up. Seeing the monkey struggle made the Dragon King smile, but just as he did, Sun Wukong burst into laughter and threw the mighty weapon into the air as if it was a feather. "This is truly the heaviest you have? It feels like a comb. Don't you have anything heavier?"

Now the Dragon King was truly desperate. He needed to be rid of this monkey. He couldn't stand being ridiculed anymore. Just then his wife swam into the hall and whispered in his ear, "There's a pillar that's been glowing for the past few days, perhaps it is fated to be the monkey's."

Together, they all swam to see this pillar. It was located deep in the palace in a courtyard. Sun Wukong's eyes lit with real joy when he saw it. The pillar was massive and towered upwards beyond what they could see. It was wide, and even hugging it, Sun Wukong could not grasp his arms fully around it.

The Dragon King started to whisper to his wife. "Will anything happen if he actually does manage to take it? The pillar is there for the stability of the sea."

"It's mostly symbolic," she said.

Just then, Sun Wukong lifted the pillar up and swung it around, but his movements were awkward and barely controlled. The royal couple had to quickly dodge and swim to the side to avoid getting struck.

"Perhaps it should be a little smaller," Sun Wukong muttered to himself. Immediately, the pillar shrank to the size of a long fighting stick. The Monkey King laughed with delight. This truly was the weapon for him. He rapidly spun and twirled it around, trying out his moves. The weapon moved with such fury that huge water currents formed and nearly swept away the entire court.

Sun Wukong laughed again and then changed the pole's shape. First it became big, then small, then medium, before he finally made it as small as a needle and tucked it behind his ear, ready for any future battle.

Upsetting Heaven

Armed with his new weapon and shiny golden, impenetrable armor (a gift from the Dragon King to ensure the monkey would leave), Sun Wukong explored the world in search for immortality and because he wanted to show the world what he could do. First, he encountered demons and immortals and overwhelmed them all, either through force or simple mischief and nuisance. Eventually, the king of the underworld heard of him and decided to capture him. He managed to kidnap the monkey while he was sleeping but regretted his action as soon as Sun Wukong woke up.

Seeing that he was in the underworld, Sun Wukong decided to make the best of it. With his pole always in his hand, he fought his way free from all of the guards and then started to look for the book of the judge, the book that the king of the underworld owned. Unmatched in speed and illusion, Sun Wukong eventually found the book deep in the underworld. Turning the pages, he finally saw his own name. Written after it were the words, *Dies at the age of 342.* He quickly erased his name, thinking that this should ensure his immortality. He left the underworld, happy knowing that he had finally obtained immortality.

This action upset all of the other immortals, of course. Never before had anyone simply struck out their name from the book to become eternal. Immortality was something earned, something given to those that had achieved greatness or who had learned the most important lessons in life. The king of the underworld complained that his dominion had been defiled and that the Monkey King had robbed him of one of his powers.

The Jade Emperor was also upset and decided to take action. He had heard of the monkey's exploits and knew that direct confrontation should be a last resort. Instead, he invited the Monkey King up to Heaven to join the imperial palace as the Protector of the Horses of the Imperial Stables. At first, Sun Wukong was excited and happy to finally be recognized by the gods. Finally, he was getting what he and his skills deserved. However, after only a few days at his new job, he realized that the Jade Emperor was simply giving him a task to keep him occupied and out of mischief. He had become nothing more than a horse groom.

Sun Wukong was furious and decided to revolt. Heaven's warriors were sent out to fight him but proved to be no match. Sun Wukong stood firm, unscathed, and surrounded by disarmed and embarrassed warriors. He proclaimed himself to be the Great Sage Equal to Heaven. Now all the immortals of Heaven were angry with him, the Jade Emperor most of all. Seeing that his warriors were no match for the Monkey King, the Jade Emperor tried to calm and appease Sun Wukong with a new title and gave him the honor of guarding the peach orchards. Sun Wukong accepted this and calmed down, but still continued to call himself the Great Sage Equal to Heaven.

One day, the Queen-Empress was having a banquet with all the deities, but the Great Sage Equal to Heaven was not on the list to be invited. Sun Wukong soon found out and was yet again furious. He started his tantrum by eating all the peaches in the peach orchard, which are not regular peaches, but peaches of immortality, giving himself immortality a second time. This was not enough for him. Knowing that everyone was at the party, the Monkey King sneaked into Laozi's quarter, the great Taoist founder himself, and stole a few of his pills of immortality. Having ensured his immortality thrice over, he felt ready to challenge Heaven. He crashed the party turning over tables, drinking the imperial wine, and challenging all who dared to oppose him. A few of the deities tried to take control and fight him, but to no avail. The Jade Emperor ordered 100,000 warriors to take him down. Alone, Sun Wukong still won, his pole becoming every size it needed to take his opponents down.

The great deities then saw what the Monkey King had done to the orchard, and Laozi realized that his house has been plundered. Laozi and the three-eyed Er Lang Shen joined forces with the rest of Heaven and managed to subdue and capture the monkey at last. They tried to kill him with fire, axes, and poison, but nothing worked. Sun Wukong was unkillable and a true immortal. Laozi then threw Sun Wukong into the Eight Trigram Furnace, hoping that would kill him. But even after 49 days of the most excruciating fires, searing flames, and alchemy of the Taoist scholars, the monkey remained alive. He was sizzling, but unscathed and still as dangerous. In fact, he was even more dangerous, as the fires had given him incredible vision that could penetrate and see through anything. Sun Wukong burst free and challenged the gods once again, daring anyone to face him.

Heaven was desperate, as none of the gods could best the Monkey King. The Jade Emperor pleaded with the Buddha, the greatest being in the universe, to help them. The Buddha came and talked to Sun Wukong, holding him in his palm.

"Why do you wish to rule over Heaven?" the Buddha asked the monkey.

"I am the most powerful creature in the whole universe," he answered. "I can beat any of the deities here in Heaven. I am the strongest and I can jump thousands of miles in only one jump, being anywhere I want to in an instant."

"If you are so strong, then I challenge you to a dare."

The monkey was instantly excited. He excelled at challenges. He was the best. "I accept," Sun Wukong said, without hesitation.

"I want to see if you can jump out of my hand. It should be easy for you. After all, you can jump thousands of miles."

The Monkey King laughed and jumped to the edge of the universe. Five pillars surrounded him and he peed on them to mark that he had been there. Then he jumped back, ready to gloat. But nothing changed. Instead, the pillars became Buddha's five fingers. In fact, he had never left Buddha's hand. Sun Wukong had been defeated and as punishment for all the havoc he had caused, Buddha trapped him under the mountain where he had come from. For five hundred years, the Monkey King was trapped and left to think over all of what he had done.

Sun Wukong - The Buddhist Disciple

Time passed and the Monkey King was kept under the mountain, locked away from the world to ensure that he would cause no mischief. A Buddhist monk, who had been thrown out of Heaven and was doing penance for his sins, was now in his tenth lifetime. This time he was asked to go on a mission to the west to find sacred Buddhist scriptures and bring them into China. The monk's name was XuanZang, or Tang Seng. China had changed and moved into the Tang dynasty, where the roads were dangerous and things were not as they once were. The monk was frail and unequipped to go alone on this perilous journey. Guan Yin, the Goddess of Mercy, knew this and asked Buddha what they could do. He asked Heaven for the permission to release Sun Wukong to be the monk's protector. Heaven agreed, not able to argue against the Buddha. Besides, the Buddha was not simply going to release the mischievous Monkey King without precautions. He created a magical golden headband that would go on Sun Wukong's head which would allow Tang Seng to control him. If the Monkey King tried to do anything that was not permitted or was displeasing to Tang Seng, he would feel paralyzing pain in his head, utterly disabling him. Buddha and Guan Yin hoped that this journey to the west would teach both Tang Seng and Sun Wukong lessons and help them find the true meaning of being a Buddhist.

As soon as Sun Wukong was set free, he felt the golden headband on his head and tried to remove it, but instantly felt pain that filled his entire being. With the pain searing through him, he was thrown to the ground and unable to move. He submitted to Tang Seng and agreed to join him in the recovery of the texts. Together, they encountered 81 tribulations and trials, fought demons and temptations, and became better beings.

Early in their journey, they met two other characters who joined their cause.

Pigsy (Zhu Bajie)

One of the admirals of heaven, one of many of the deities that Sun Wukong had fought and beaten when he caused havoc in heaven, was flawed to a high degree. Zhu Bajie was in charge of 80,000 sailors, but would often get drunk, eat far too much, and try to seduce and sleep with young maidens and other women; in other words, he was far too easily swayed by all the sins of the flesh. One day, he saw the moon goddess Chang'e pass by. He was already drunk and found her beauty intoxicating. Zhu Bajie advanced towards her, flirted, and tried to force her into sleeping with him. This was the final act that condemned him, and he was instantly banished from Heaven and sent to Earth in the form of a pig with human capabilities. Pigsy, as he was now known due to his form, was huge, fat, and had all the features of a pig, but could walk on two legs, talk, and fight. Everyone shied away from him for he was an abomination and looked monstrous. He made a home for himself in a cave, but ventured into villages for food.

One day, the goddess Guan Yin passed by, looking for people to protect Tang Seng on his journey to find the sacred scriptures. Seeing Pigsy in the cave, she stopped.

"Do you wish for redemption, to atone for your past and become better?" she asked him.

He bowed down on the ground. "Yes, I do. I am repentant," he said.

"A monk and a monkey will pass here soon. You will become a monk and join them as their companion."

"Yes, goddess," he said.

With that, Guan Yin disappeared.

A few months later, Sun Wukong and Tang Seng passed by a village near Pigsy's cave. There they saw a monstrous pig-like being dragging a young girl. "I will marry you," he shouted, as the girl cried, struggling against the big pig-beast. Tang Seng quickly gave his assent to allow Sun Wukong to intervene. The Monkey King somersaulted next to the pig and hit him hard in the chest. Pigsy dropped the girl, furious at the intervention. He roared and tried to ram the monkey, but Sun Wukong laughed and jumped into the air, appearing behind the pig and kicking him hard on his backside. Pigsy squealed in pain and became red in his face. He tried to fight again, but now Sun Wukong had lost his patience. He took out his fighting pole, made it large, and swept Pigsy onto his back. Then he leaped close, pinning him down.

"What do we do with people who cannot control their lust?" he asked Tang Seng the monk.

"We teach them control," the monk answered. "Let him go."

Sun Wukong did as he was told, fearing the pain of the golden headband, but he kept a careful eye on Pigsy who was still scarlet in his face. He bowed to the monk and finally to the monkey. Just then, Guan Yin appeared again.

"This is your other companion," she told Tang Seng. Sun Wukong stared at her in astonishment, insulted that his protection was not enough and that this pig was to now join them.

Tang Seng merely bowed his head at her, ever tranquil. And so, they became three and they set out on their journey to the west.

Sandy (Sha Wujing)

Not long after Pigsy joined Tang Seng and Sun Wukong, they came to a long, massive river. Not only was it impassable, it was also guarded by a terrible, fierce beast who feasted on any humans who strayed too close. But this was the path that the companions had to take on their pilgrimage and they needed the monster to be able to cross the river, as no one else would be able to bring them across.

As Pigsy and Tang Seng approached the river, the massive fish monster leaped out of the water and became an ogre. He had red, matted hair, a long magical staff in his hand, and a necklace of nine skulls around his neck. He attacked and Pigsy tried to fight him. For a while they were locked in combat, each trying to strike each other and both able to deflect each other too well. Even when a hit actually landed, neither seemed to care, but continued fighting. Sun Wukong, whose sight allowed him to see the work of demons and witches, was away fighting a demon, but when he finally appeared, the ogre immediately turned into a fish and jumped back into the river. Even this fish-ogre had heard of Sun Wukong and knew he would meet his match.

However, as soon as the Monkey King disappeared on another mission, the ogre returned and began to fight Pigsy yet again. It became clear that Pigsy could not defeat him, but neither could the monster defeat Pigsy. Sun Wukong appeared and again the ogre instantly jumped back into the river as a great fish. This time though, Sun Wukong created a copy of himself and pretended to leave, while he waited for the ogre to show up again. As soon as the ogre reappeared on land, Sun Wukong fought him and forced him into submission.

Again, Guan Yin appeared.

"This is Sandy and he shall be your fourth and final companion. Together you will all make the journey to find the sacred scriptures," she said, before turning to the ogre. "You shall redeem yourself in this quest. Your punishment will no longer pursue you here on Earth as long as you devote yourself to this pilgrimage and complete it."

He bowed and thanked her. With that, she disappeared.

"What did you do?" Pigsy asked.

"Once, I was a general in Heaven. But one day, I accidentally knocked over the Queen Empress' goblet, shattering it. With that, I lost my title and was banished to Earth in this grotesque form." As he said that, he gained his human features back, his red hair changing into black. He laughed happily. "I am grateful for this quest of yours and this opportunity."

"She mentioned a punishment that pursued you?" the Monkey King asked, gazing intently at him.

"I live in a river to hide. Before being thrown out, I was whipped 800 times and then cursed. Every day here on Earth swords would come down and stab me, but they cannot reach me in the river. It was my one refuge."

The Monkey King nodded, but there was clear anger in his eyes. Then he put his hands to his temples, rubbing them as if a faint buzz of pain had whispered to him for even thinking that the gods were unjust.

"Please, now that you are with us, help us cross the river," Tang Seng said.

Sandy brought forth a gourd, which he turned into a boat for them to cross in and so they continued on their pilgrimage for the sacred texts.

Author's Note:

The legend of the Monkey King is well-known and perhaps the most famous of all of China's legends, which is why it has been given a bit more space in this book. It shows the clear multi-layers of thought and beliefs that exist in Chinese mythology. At first, we see that the Monkey King is a devout Taoist student. That said, he does not really help people with his skills, which is a failure in that belief, but he does master himself and his body and ultimately achieves immortality-the greatest possible achievement for any Taoist. We are meant to read him as being too arrogant and chaotic in the Chinese literary classic *The Journey to the West*, where Sun Wukong must learn to control himself and serve the Buddhistic purpose. It is also from this book and this movement towards Buddhism within China and Chinese thought that Buddha is emphasized as the ultimate being, even above the Jade Emperor and Laozi. However, even within this Chinese Buddhistic text, we still see all the elements of old Chinese mythology—there are demons and deities and most of the companions and even enemies have been brought in from other tales of old and then remade into this narrative.

Sun Wukong is easy to love because he is incredibly talented and brilliant but also mischievous and unpredictable. He has been drafted into computer games, modern animated series, and movies and will most likely continue to be a cultural icon in China.

Chapter 6 – The Investiture of the Gods

King Zhou's Hubris

During the Shang dynasty, around 1100 BC, the kings were harsher and crueler. One king was called Da Yi, and he had three sons. One day, he was walking in the garden and admiring its beauty. Suddenly, a corner of the pavilion fell. Thankfully, his youngest son, Prince Zhou, was there to catch it, supporting it with his bare hands. The ministers and advisers were all impressed and told the king to make his youngest son the next king, as he would have the strength to rule the kingdom.

However, physical strength is not enough to run a kingdom and when Zhou became king he showed that he was also cruel and foolhardy. He waged war and was successful, but his ministers started to warn him that his successes would soon cease unless he paid homage to the gods. King Zhou followed the advice he was given and went to the temple of Nüwa. He placed his incense by the altar and murmured a quick prayer. Suddenly, a draft blew through the temple and the great curtain that veiled the depiction of the goddess was swept away. Her form, which was never meant to be seen by mere mortals, was revealed. The illustration of her was a masterful piece, portraying her as the woman of all women, as femininity itself. King Zhou was instantly smitten and filled with lust for her. He gaped and stared in awe at her.

"Oh Nüwa, most glorious and beautiful of all women. I hunger for you and need you by my side. If only you were made of flesh, I would marry you this instant."

He kept staring and would not avert his eyes. His ministers and guards were all horrified but dared not lift their eyes in case they too would see Nüwa and dishonor her.

The king broke the silence again and turned to his men: "Quick, get me brushes and ink. I must write a poem to her so she may hear me and meet with me."

His servants could not but obey and soon he was brought the ink he required. King Zhou began to write on the walls of the temple.

Her beauty unmatched, even as fashions of clay and paint,

Forms and figures to make any man want for her,

Fruits which are ripe and firm, with a garden most lush.

Would she only be in flesh, I would have her in my palace.

The ministers were horrified both by the writing now on the wall and by its contents. One of them spoke out:

"My king, I am but your humble servant, but please, Nüwa has always protected our people. She is a goddess and far above our humble station. This poem is an affront. She will not view it lightly and ill will fall upon our kingdom."

"Nonsense," the king said, still full of lust, but with a hint of underlying anger. "This poem is praise to her beauty and all should see it. It is my gift to her and the kingdom. I will hear no more of it."

After that, no one dared to speak, but all trembled in fear of what was to come.

Nüwa's Rage

When Nüwa came back from her trip and arrived at her temple, she saw the blasphemous poem and screamed with rage. She immediately flew down to the palace to kill King Zhou on the spot for his arrogance and dishonor. However, as soon as she saw him, she could see the tendrils of time around him – she saw his fortune, his future and his past. He was to reign twenty-eight more years, as had been decided by Heaven long ago when his ancestor won centuries of luck. She stopped her wrath and knew she would find her revenge through other means.

She summoned three spirits to her temple and sent them forth to bring harm and downfall to King Zhou, but they were to hurt no one else. Should they succeed, she would give them human bodies and life.

Meanwhile, in the palace, King Zhou could think of nothing but Nüwa's beauty. It consumed him day and night. He dreamt of her and thought of her and his kingdom suffered. Ministers that he had always listened to now seemed foolish to him and he begun to appreciate the flattery of fools more. When two of these ministers of flattery came to him, he shared his struggle with them.

"Nothing has purpose or meaning anymore. Nothing compares to Nüwa's beauty. What can I do?" he asked.

"My king," they said. "You must send out a message to all your dukes and ministers. Ask them for the most beautiful girls in the land. With a thousand young maidens to choose a concubine from, you will no longer be lusting over any other beauty."

Their advice made sense to the king and he asked for the decree to go out.

Many of the dukes and ministers were outraged. The king already had a wife and two concubines along with a thousand beautiful women that served him. Surely, he had no need for anymore. All of them knew how much this would upset the people. One of them spoke up and convinced the king to take back his decree. Trusting the minister, who had served his father very well, King Zhou finally agreed to withdraw the decree.

A few years later, it was time for all the dukes and ministers to visit and give gifts. One of them was a straightforward and honest man who did not like the flattering ministers that held the king's ear. These ministers did not like him either and they told the king that this duke, Su Hu, had a most beautiful daughter and taking her as his concubine would not upset the people, as it would be only one woman rather than a thousand. The king liked the idea and sent the message to Su Hu to bring his daughter, as he wanted to see her famed beauty. Su Hu refused and war ensued, but after a few battles, Su Hu gave in and brought himself and his daughter to the palace. On the way there, they were attacked by a vixen spirit, one of the three spirits that had been sent by Nüwa, who killed Su Hu's daughter and took her place.

When they came to the palace, the king was furious to see Su Hu still alive and wanted him executed.

"He has brought his daughter; she is just outside." The king's other ministers advised. "See if she pleases the king's eye first, and if so, pardon Su Hu as he was always a good, loyal duke prior to this incident."

The king agreed and as his eyes fell on Daji, the fox spirit, he fell deeply in love. She was fairer than the fairest summer's eve. Her movements were graceful and she swayed like a cherry blossom in the breeze. He was filled with blind lust for her and instantly pardoned Su Hu. Then he took Daji into his arms, locked eyes with her, and was mesmerized. He asked for the servants to take her to his palace. After they had washed and oiled her, he soon joined her in his palace quarters and they did not leave the room for three months. No one saw the king. Every moment he was awake he spent with Daji, enchanted by her body and looks. The reports were piling in. War had broken out with giants and monsters. Famine had struck the east. But the king stayed in his palace with Daji, indulging in wine and lust, while Nüwa laughed at his decline.

Author's note:

The Investiture of the Gods is a long tale, and this is merely a short extract which shows how it starts. After many battles and many deeds, the tale ends with numerous heroes being exalted into heaven as immortals, thus forming a pantheon of gods, which is how the book got its name. The book is a compilation of myths and legends surrounding this tumultuous time and shows the rise of the Taoist immortals.

Chapter 7 – Three Kingdoms

All things united must eventually divide, and all things divided will eventually unite. The Han dynasty had ruled for a long time, but with the ascension of Emperor Huang, their decline began. He deposed and humiliated many lords, governors, and nobles. Instead, he elevated eunuchs and put them in new positions of power, giving them more and more influence. Other warlords and people were getting angry as corruption spread through the palace and the country. However, nothing happened for a while, and soon Emperor Huang passed away to be replaced by Emperor Ling. Emperor Ling was too young to rule in his own right when he came to power, so Dou Wu, who oversaw the military, and Chen Fan, who oversaw education, ruled in his stead and advised him. They saw the negative influence that the eunuchs had and wanted to end it by plotting the assassination of the chief eunuch. Sadly, it was noticed in time, and instead they were assassinated, which only continued the decline of the Han dynasty.

At this time, crazy incidents began to occur all over the country. Storms were far more frequent, the seas raged in unexpected ways, attacking even the coastal villages in ways they never had before, earthquakes struck towns, and even worse, supernatural incidents took place. The first of these happened to the young emperor himself. He walked into a room to relax and suddenly, with a breeze, a green coiled snake flew in the window and landed on his chair. Emperor Ling was so frightened that he fainted on the spot. His attendants took him away, removing the snake too. In the villages, female hens suddenly turned into male roosters. Rivers flooded, winds blew the wrong directions and there were thunderstorms without any rain. The emperor was terrified and still so young that he did not know what to do. He sent out an edict asking all his advisers what these signs could mean and why they were happening.

One of these advisers was brutally blunt and sent a letter for the emperor's eyes only, blaming it all on the fact that the emperor and the country was ruled by women and eunuchs. However, one of the eunuchs found the letter and read it before it reached the emperor. As soon as the eunuchs read the letter, they began to plot. In no time, they had forced the adviser to be banished and sent to his hometown, removing him from court. After that, the government sunk further into decline and bandits started appearing all over the land as people began to revolt.

At this time, Zhang Jiao, a dissident, met an old man while he was up in the mountains. The man had a long beard and carried a walking stick in one hand and a big tome in the other. This book was called *The Essential Art of Great Peace*, and the man gave it to Zhang Jiao, telling him to study it to achieve peace in the land. The man said he was an immortal sent to give him this book. Zhang Jiao read the book and shared its secrets with his two brothers. The three of them became healers and healed people throughout the land, but it was said that Zhang Jiao could also control weather and much more, as he had become a great sorcerer. Zhang Jiao and his brothers had seen the decline of the kingdom. They decided that the emperor had lost his Mandate of Heaven and that it was time for a new era. This sparked a rebellion which was bloody and gruesome.

Eventually, the emperor's forces vanquished the rebellion under He Jin, the emperor's general. But during this time, Emperor Ling had passed away, possibly assassinated but no one could pinpoint who had been behind it. He Jin placed a new emperor to serve as a figurehead. The eunuchs saw that He Jin was getting far too powerful and did not like this. They feared that soon he would depose them and strip their power, so they had him assassinated. At his death, He Jin's followers rebelled and fought against the eunuchs and their forces. During the commotion, the emperor fled.

A warlord, Dong Zhuo, found him and took back the imperial city from both He Jin's followers and the eunuchs. He placed the emperor back in power and claimed he had taken the city back for him; but of course, Dong Zhuo held the real power as ruler. He claimed to be protecting the emperor, but soon deposed him and found another child emperor to use as a puppet instead. Dong Zhuo ruled as a tyrant and the land continued to suffer. Attempts were made to assassinate him, but they failed.

One of these assassination attempts was made by a warrior and general called Cao Cao. After his failed effort, he was forced to flee, but he managed to build up a band of followers and warriors. He sent out a fake imperial decree, in which he told all the warlords about Dong Zhuo keeping the emperor as a prisoner and how this tyranny needed to end. The warlords went into alliance with Cao Cao to free the emperor, and together they began to fight back against Dong Zhuo and his persecution. Big battles took place and Cao Cao and his forces won them all, pushing Dong Zhuo back.

Dong Zhuo soon realized that he was fighting a losing battle and retreated from the capital, leaving the emperor there. Instead, he tried to find a stronger defense in his own hometown. Alas, surrounded by family in his own fortress, his son killed him.

Meanwhile, Cao Cao had captured the capital and now had the emperor in his care, who he claimed to protect. In reality, the emperor was still a figurehead, just with a new master puppeteer.

Now, we must travel back in time to visit a young man called Liu Bei. Liu Bei had seen the rebellion take place and the havoc that Zhang Jiao had caused. Liu Bei had always been special and knew that he was sent from heaven. He could trace his lineage many centuries back to Emperor Jing—he was in the line of Heaven's chosen rulers. As Liu Bei saw this rebellion against the imperial family by Zhang Jiao the sorcerer, he was outraged and gathered his own people around him to fight against the uprising. He helped He Jin and the imperial forces to vanquish the rebels, but after the rebellion had been crushed, Liu Bei received hardly any recognition. He was made prefect of a little country, but with the vast amount of corruption present in government, he declined the post.

Liu Bei instead kept fighting; he fought against Dong Zhuo, Dong Zhuo's son, and eventually against Cao Cao.

During the reign of Cao Cao's emperor, the Han kingdom continued its civil war and its decline. In the midst of the chaos, Cao Cao gathered his army to try and reunite China. He battled against Liu Bei and another warlord called Sun Quan, who had been taking territory in the east. Liu Bei and Sun Quan won.

With Cao Cao's death, all pretense of an emperor ruling China was stripped away since his son, Cao Pi, decided to proclaim himself as emperor. Of course, Liu Bei and Sun Quan disagreed, both holding large areas of land in China. They too declared themselves to be kings, and eventually emperors, of their land. Thus, three kingdoms were born and the land was broken in three.

Author's note:

"Three Kingdoms" is multi-faceted. It is a historical period of time where the country was split into three kingdoms, and it is also a work of literature in the form of *The Romance of the Three Kingdoms*, which weaves together orally kept legends, myths, and history.

This story, along with *The Investiture of the Gods*, showcases what it means to lose the Mandate of Heaven, which is an incredibly important concept in China, even today. It means that the ruling authorities are seen to be chosen by Heaven and are meant to rule. However, as soon as the kingdom is in decline and there are signs that show disfavor from Heaven, it means that the Mandate has been broken which in turn allows for rebellion and revolt. This idea is also shown in the Monkey King story; because the Jade Emperor and the Taoist pantheon could not defeat Sun Wukong, their time had passed and this showed the necessity of Buddhism and how it had become the dominant belief at that time.

Chapter 8 – Modern Mythology – The Bottle Gourd Children

Once upon a time, an old man was climbing in the mountains searching for herbs with healing powers. He stumbled upon a mountain that was shaped exactly like a bottle gourd. As he was climbing, he tripped and fell. What he did not know was that in his fall he had freed two evil spirits that had been locked underneath the mountain for a long time. One was female with the body of a snake, while the other was a man with aspects of a scorpion. Both of them had magical powers and immediately began to terrorize the nearby villages as they had done before they had been captured.

Fortunately, the mountain also kept the secret to recapturing the demons and defeating them for good. Deep inside it was a bottle gourd which radiated with every color of the rainbow. The old man managed to find it and retrieved a seed from it. When he got the seed, the mountain itself cracked open in half. He took the seed home and planted it. The next day, it had already grown into a bottle gourd vine.

The vine had grown seven bottle gourds on it, all of them of different colors. They grew at different speeds, but all were healthily growing and all had a unique color.

While the gourds grew, the demons rejoiced at their freedom, feasting on food taken from the villages. They also gathered other creatures and demons to join them. Every now and then, they would take on their serpent and scorpion form to terrorize the area further.

The snake-woman demon had a specific artifact that allowed her to summon magical weapons. One day, she used it to produce a mirror and scouted the land around her. Looking through her mirror, she saw the bottle gourd vine and how it was growing. The bottle gourd vine struck fear in her heart so she sent minions to attack it. A whole swarm of demon bees came to kill the vine with their poison, but one of the gourds, the green one, blew fire and killed them all.

The snake demon then sent a fire-breathing snake to attack them, but as it tried to burn the vine down, the blue gourd spouted water to save them.

The old man was watching from his window, and seeing the snake attack the vine, he went out to kill it. As soon as he left his house, the snake demon was there to capture him and take him away.

None of the bottle gourds were ripe yet so they hung helplessly on the vine as the old man was dragged away.

The Red Bottle Gourd

The next day, the red bottle gourd shook viciously. Then with a loud crack, it tore in half and out came a red-dressed boy. He was the eldest of the children and was called Big Brother. All the bottle gourd children were strong, fast, and could jump high, but Big Brother was particularly strong and had a special ability that allowed him to change size, growing huge when he wanted to. Big Brother went to the nearby village and saw the destruction that raged. Everywhere there were bones and decay, and the farms and houses had all been burnt. He traveled past the villages into the mountains to attack the demons and bring back the old man. As soon as he came to the mountain, a big rock fell and tried to crush him, but he lifted it up and threw it away. He continued to wander the mountains until he spotted a cave. Inside, he found the scorpion and snake demons and told them to give back the old man or he would destroy their cave.

"You can't destroy our cave because your old man is here too," said the snake woman. "Let me take you to him and you can see him."

Big Brother, not being the brightest gourd, followed her. There he saw the old man lying on a stone table. He ran to the old man to bring him back home, but as soon as he touched the man, the old man disappeared and the whole place turned into quicksand. He was trapped and could not escape, nor were his powers any help.

The snake woman and scorpion man decided to keep the boy trapped to lure the rest of the children to them too, so that they could capture and kill all of them together.

The Orange Bottle Gourd

The next day, the orange gourd began to shake and out came an orange child. This child had supervision and hearing. Even from their house, he could see his trapped brother deep in the mountain. The orange child had to be much more careful and rely on his wits, since he had no real physical powers. He traveled to the mountains and lured the guards away with some treats. Once inside the cave, the second child looked for a way to get rid of the snake woman's artifact, but it was hidden away behind an impenetrable rock. Looking for a way to get past the rock, he traveled into a deep cavern where the snake woman had put up two giant mirrors. There, he was blinded by the reflections they caused. His eyes screamed in pain and then the snake demon came out and struck his ears too. No longer could he see or hear, and she threw him into prison with the old man.

The Yellow Bottle Gourd

In prison, they were found by a mole creature who dug them out of the mountain. The demons soon realized that the second brother and the old man had fled and pursued them. As the scorpion man caught up to recapture them, a yellow bottle gourd appeared. It still wasn't open. The scorpion demon tried to cut it in half, but instead that produced the yellow brother, whose superpower was invincibility. He easily withstood the scorpion man's attacks, allowing the second brother and the old man to escape home. The yellow brother attacked the scorpion man back, and his fingers shattered the scorpion's claws and sword. The demon fled, teleporting with a wisp of black smoke behind him. The third brother was not easily daunted, however, and chased after, back into the mountain. There he punched through the gates, his hands harder than any steel or iron. He found the mirror of the demons that had allowed them to see the gourd children growing on the vine and destroyed it.

The snake woman appeared, furious. She tried to attack the yellow child, but he laughed at her, letting her hit him with her sword.

"Bring out all your weapons. I will destroy them all," he said, laughing.

"If you can withstand three of my attacks, I will free your first brother and surrender," the snake demon said.

The boy laughed again. "Easy. Try your best." He bent his neck forward.

The snake woman brought out a new sword and struck him. Nothing happened.

"Is that the best you have?" the boy taunted. "You might as well surrender and give me my brother now."

She hit him again, but to no avail.

He laughed at her. "Last try."

This time the sword bent and turned into thousands of stringy swords, and rather than hit the third brother, they wrapped around him, tying him up. His invulnerability was no help against this, and the demons locked him up deep in the mountain.

The Green and Blue Bottle Gourd

The next day, two children were born, both the green and the blue one. The blue one immediately began watering the vine to ensure the others could keep growing. Once finished with this task, the two gourds turned to the task of freeing their brothers. This time, however, the old man cautioned them from going against the demons by themselves. Instead, they were to find herbs that could heal the second brother's hearing and sight. That way, they could get information on where the other brothers were now hidden and what the demons were doing.

The green and blue brothers headed out to look for herbs and saw the famine in the land. Everywhere, there was destruction and dry land. The blue child watered it, while the green one set fire to all the pests and snakes that were terrorizing the area.

Meanwhile, the demons were looking for an ancient magical pot that would allow them to destroy the bottle gourd children. Deep in a lake, they found the pot, but when they fished it out, it spurted fire and nearly destroyed them.

The two children saw the fire in the mountain and ran towards it. The blue brother quickly sent water at the flames to extinguish it, while the fire brother sucked some of it into himself. Then they saw the demons who were happy to have survived the fire.

"We must thank you, children," they said. "You have saved us."

"We can set you ablaze again," the green gourd child said.

"No need," the snake woman said, "why not let us thank you instead? We shall have a feast to celebrate this glorious day."

"Release our brothers too."

"Of course, of course," the demons said.

The children were persuaded and followed the demons back to the mountain.

When they got to the mountain, the demons led them past a place where water blocked their path.

"We used to go across here, but it flooded yesterday," the snake woman said. "We will have to take the long way around."

"Nonsense," the blue brother said and opened his mouth and sucked the water into himself, allowing them to pass.

They arrived deep into the cave where the demons had a feast prepared.

"Your hall is very cold," the green fire child said. "I will fix that." Fire poured out of his mouth and all the torches and hearths were lit.

"You are both so impressive. Your skills rival that of the gods," the serpent demon said. "To celebrate your skills, let us drink wine together."

She produced a goblet filled with wine from her artifact and passed it to the green brother. He drained the glass and instantly began to wobble.

"The wine was cold," he slurred and then fell sound asleep.

"Brother!" the blue brother exclaimed.

"Wow, one glass of wine and he got drunk and fell asleep," the scorpion man mocked.

"Try me then!" the blue brother said. "Give me all your wine."

The scorpion demon and snake woman opened up all their barrels of wine, and the blue brother simply sat in his seat and summoned it all into his mouth. In a few moments, all their wine was gone.

"Huh, is that all you have? I hardly had time to taste the wine before it was gone," the blue brother said.

The scorpion demon was outraged. "He emptied all our wine!" The snake lady looked at the child, horrified, trying to think quickly of a new plan to fool the child. She asked her magical artifact for a new weapon to use and a massive bowl appeared. In the bowl was a new, sweet, fragrant wine.

"Mmm," the blue boy said, "that smells like wonderful wine."

"Let's make a deal then," the snake lady said. "If you can drain this bowl, we will give you anything you want."

"Easy," the water brother said and summoned the wine to him again. It flowed right into his open mouth. The bowl was emptied, and the blue brother began to sway. Before he could even look to see how much he had drunk, the bowl had refilled. He emptied it again and again until he finally collapsed, knocked out from all the alcohol.

The demons laughed, and the snake lady instantly took out her artifact to freeze the fire brother so that he would not be able to awaken and escape. The blue brother she enchanted and locked away in the deep wine bowl.

The Dark Blue Bottle Gourd

The next day, back at the house, birds flew in with the magical plant that the second brother needed to restore his sight and hearing. A few drops of nectar were dropped into his eyes and ears and suddenly his senses were restored. Just as this happened, an evil wind came and the demons appeared. The scorpion demon quickly attacked the old man and sent him tumbling off a cliff, while demonic bat minions attacked the second brother, capturing him with a net. The snake lady laughed and plucked the last two bottle gourds off the vine before they could hatch.

The demons quickly captured the second brother and brought everyone, including the unborn gourds, back to their cave and decided they would find a way to turn the bottle gourd children into an immortality potion. But two of the bottle gourds were still not ripe.

"Maybe we could grow them into our children," the snake demon said and placed the vine over a well of blackness and evil. But as soon as she did, the sixth bottle gourd jumped off the vine and cracked open.

But nothing appeared. Suddenly, the demons were being kicked and punched, before realizing that the child had the power of invisibility. The child ran away before they could find him.

Meanwhile, the old man, who had been thrown off a cliff, was awakened by an eagle. The bird took him on its wings and flew him to the bottle gourd mountain. There, the mountain spoke to him.

"You have awakened almost all of the seven bottle gourd children, but you forgot to take the Rainbow Lotus. Without it, they cannot combine their powers and defeat the demons. I will let you go back into me and find it. Take it to them and help them save the land."

"The children have already been destroyed by the demons. It's too late!" the old man said.

"They are not dead yet, merely captured. Go. Find the Rainbow Lotus and bring it to them."

A cloud appeared and the old man stepped onto it. It flew into the mountain and took him to its heart, where he could see a Rainbow Lotus flower waiting for him. He took it and was quickly transported out of the mountain.

During this time, the old man flew home on the eagle, Rainbow Lotus in hand. He found the home destroyed, with none of the bottle gourds left. Instead, several demonic minions had been waiting for his arrival. They trapped him and took him back to the demons' cave.

Back in the demon's lair, the seventh brother was still in its gourd, hanging over the well of darkness. There the demons cultivated it, speaking to it and pouring evil ointments on it, trying to make it theirs.

Meanwhile, the dark blue brother explored the demons' mountain and found all of his brothers but couldn't free any of them. Finally, he found his second brother and asked for his help to find the snake lady's artifact.

"The scorpion demon is holding it," the second brother revealed. "He is asleep right now but might wake soon. It seems the demons always keep it on themselves."

"I will find a way to get it," the dark blue brother said.

The sixth brother was still sneaking around in the demons' mountain and found the scorpion demon feasting on wine and food. He used his invisibility and caused the demon to spill his meal multiple times. Then he teased and taunted the scorpion man. The demon was outraged and told all of his minions to catch him. The snake lady arrived and she too joined the chase. All of them tried to catch the dark blue child, but he evaded them, constantly changing where he was. Not even nets or frost worked to catch him, as he dodged them and instead made the snake demon accidentally freeze the scorpion man. As she had tried to freeze him, she had used the incantation needed to use the artifact. She quickly melted him, using the same incantation, which the dark blue brother heard. Both of the demons and their minions were outraged and looked everywhere for the dark blue child but could not find him.

Eventually, the demons had tired and went to sleep, holding their precious artifact in their hands. The dark blue brother waited until they were fast asleep. He took a leaf from his clothes and tickled it across the scorpion man's nose to make him sneeze. As the scorpion sneezed, he dropped the artifact he had been carefully holding. Before it hit the floor, the sixth child picked it up. He quickly ran to where all of his brothers were hidden and unfroze the green brother, released the yellow one from his ropes, and saved the others from their traps.

The Violet Bottle Gourd

The six brothers went to find the last violet brother who was encapsulated in a black prison, above a dark cauldron of evil.

"We are here to save you, brother!" they said.

"Brother? I don't have any brother. Go away or I'll call on Mummy!" he said, still inside his bottle gourd.

The brothers left him and started to attack the minions to find the demons and finally deal with them, once and for all.

However, the old man had finally arrived and was brought to the demons and the snake demon and scorpion man took him to see the seventh child. Just then, the violet child was born out of his bottle gourd. Unlike his brothers, his gourd did not break, but instead he was summoned out of it. The gourd shrunk and the child kept it in his hands for it was his power and weapon. He did not recognize the old man and announced his love for the snake woman, calling her mother.

"Child," she said, "we are being invaded by terrors that this man brought upon us."

"Don't worry, Mother," the boy said. "I will deal with them with my gourd."

Just then, the fourth and fifth brothers arrived.

"Release my brother and our grandpa to us," the green brother said. "Or I will spit fire at you."

"And I will drown you in water," the water brother shouted.

"Go away! How dare you attack this place?" their youngest brother shouted.

"You are confused, brother. Stop this madness," they told him.

"No, I will defend my mother and father!"

The green brother shot fire at them, but the violet brother soaked it all up into his gourd. The same happened again when the blue brother attacked with water. The violet brother was able to soak up everything and then returned fire with a spell from his gourd, causing the other two brothers to attack each other.

The red and yellow brother also arrived, but they too were made to attack each other. The violet brother then absorbed them into his bottle gourd, imprisoning them.

The orange and dark blue brother were also nearby, but were still hiding.

"I can deal with him. I still have this," the dark blue brother said, holding the demons' artifact. He went invisible and then uttered the incantation and sent it at his brother. But the seventh child's gourd absorbed it.

"Who attacks us now?" the seventh brother asked, outraged. "I will deal with them." He held out his bottle gourd and streams of water flowed out of it, finding the sixth and second brother and imprisoned them in the gourd too.

The old man openly cried. He remembered the beautiful vine he had planted with children full of potential and powers. "You have turned against your brothers," he said to the violet brother. "You don't remember anything of the care we have for you. I was your caretaker. Your grandpa."

At this, the violet brother started to cry. He could feel the truth of what the old man said and the grief resonated within him.

"He lies, child," the demons said, but there was anger in their voices.

"Mother," the violet child said, tears still in his eyes. "I have all the terrors in this bottle gourd. What do we do with them now?"

"Come, we must ensure that they never come back." The demons took the child and the old man to the pot they had found, the pot of eternal flames.

"Pour them into that," the snake demon said.

The violet boy did as he was told.

"Your bottle gourd truly is impressive," the snake lady said. "May I see it?"

"Only for a little while. It is mine," the boy said.

"Of course. I know it is yours. I would never keep it."

He handed her the gourd. Immediately, she pointed it at him and sucked him into it, before sending him into the pot of flames too.

The Rainbow Lotus

The pot burned before smoke suddenly steamed out of it and it ceased burning. Waves of water poured out and the pot stopped burning. Seeing this, the old man laughed.

"I will throw you into it too if you laugh again," the scorpion man said.

"You have caused your own failure," the old man said. "You divided the children so much that they cannot be formed into one pill of immortality and invincibility. But I can help you there. I can unite them so that they can be transformed."

"You?! Ha!" the scorpion demon mocked.

"Wait, let us see what the old man can do. What harm can it do?" the snake woman said.

At this, the old man took out the Rainbow Lotus and proclaimed, "With this the seven children can unite and become one to defeat you demons!" He threw the Rainbow Lotus toward the pot and it hovered above it, releasing drops of each color. With that, the seven boys were summoned out of the pot and into the lotus, before becoming their own size.

The demons quickly grabbed the old man, holding a knife to his throat.

"Don't hurt us or we will kill your beloved grandpa," they said.

"Don't worry about me. Just kill these demons!" the old man exclaimed.

The children hesitated and then the snake demon brought forth the youngest brother's bottle gourd.

"I will summon you back in, you terrible children!"

The old man pushed back against the scorpion demon which caught him off guard. He then lunged at the snake demon and made her drop the bottle gourd, which the violet brother quickly picked up. But before the brothers could react, the scorpion demon stabbed his blade into the back of the old man, killing him.

The brothers instantly started fighting together as one and used all of their superpowers against the demons. After the demons had been burnt, flooded, and crushed under rocks, the violet brother took out his bottle gourd and sucked them into it. As they were sucked in, the demons shrieked and shrunk into a tiny snake and scorpion. Finally, the brothers had united as one to defeat the demons and freed the land from their terror. The yellow brother split open a mountain and they locked the bottle gourd deep inside it. Then, the seven children were transformed into a rainbow mountain that stood on top of the bottle gourd. If the demons ever awaken, then so would the bottle gourd children.

Author's note:

This story is a much more recent construction from the 20th century, but uses many symbols and ideas that are taken and reshaped from mythology. The bottle gourd is traditionally thought to have healing powers in Chinese folklore; doctors have even used it to carry their medicinal herbs. It was also a symbol of Taoist immortals. This story not only uses this vegetable, but also combines it with very recognizable images, like the snake woman, who we know as Nüwa, only here she is evil. Besides this, it showcases the constant struggle between demons and humans and the importance of being careful not to disturb spirits. It also depicts the power in brotherhood and teamwork, rather than doing something by yourself.

Conclusion

Chinese mythology is as rich as it is diverse. These tales that you have read are just a selection of a vast ocean of stories, legends, and myths. This selection was made to give you a taste and hopefully leave you wanting more.

Chinese mythology is almost defined by the quest for immortality. Whether that is from Taoism, or if this idealism of immortality within Taoism stems from mythology, is hard to say. What is clear is that immortality is the greatest achievement in Chinese mythology. The gods that exist and the original Taoist pantheon became gods and achieved godhood through their action or deeds. There are, of course, exceptions to this, but they are few. Within Taoism, knowledge was the key to many things and helping other people with their knowledge of healing was especially honored.

With the arrival of Buddhism into China, immortality took a slight backseat, but the idea still remained. Buddhism brought in an element of self-control and self-denial, which is clear in the latter part of the Monkey King story. Suffering and serving penance is also emphasized.

Chinese Mythology continues to impact the society today with its ideas and ideals, even though a lot also has changed as China has become secularized. Today, you can buy the Monkey King as an ice cream and heroes from the Three Kingdoms are collectible trading cards. On a deeper level, the idea of teamwork and unity as is shown in the story of the bottle gourd children is highly cherished.

There are numerous legends, films and much more on Chinese Mythology, so if you now have a taste for a particular part of it and you want to know more, go and explore its deep caverns.

Preview of Japanese Mythology

A Captivating Guide to Japanese Folklore, Myths, Fairy Tales, Yokai, Heroes and Heroines

Introduction

The study of mythology and folklore is a peculiar one to the extent that we are looking into things which are generally regarded as untrue yet critically important to a culture. We are also taking on the study of the "lore of the folk," and this faces us with the question of exactly which folk we are talking about. Japan, of course, is a single nation, but its origins are so old and often so fragmented that unified mythology and folklore can be difficult to point to. Still, in all, there are some key texts, tales, and characters we can focus on which will give us a pretty good sense of Japanese mythology.

Japanese culture offers a wealth of religious tradition, mythology, and stunning folklore. The earliest myths found in the two main religious books, the *Kojiki* and the *Nihon Shoki*, offer the obscure and often difficult stories of the earliest creation, the birth of the islands of Japan, and the ancestral lines of the Emperors. These texts, though distant to a contemporary reader at times, are filled with bizarre stories of the magic of gods. They offer numerous gods for everything in heaven and earth. The rules of the games they play can at times be difficult to understand. Even the importance of numbers can get confusing, yet there is a logic to these texts. There is an elaborate code of conduct and an exhaustive lineage which is designed to take the reader up to the historical emperors of Japan.

It is probably important to remember as we work our way through these books that, though these are the oldest texts in Japanese mythology, they are nonetheless an amalgam of Chinese and Indian lore which found its way to Japan and mingles into the earliest beliefs of ancient Japan. If the going gets confusing, it is because the stories themselves are confusing. However, like all mythological systems, it is perhaps a mistake to try to assign a very human logic to the thoughts and actions of deities which precede humanity.

The *Kojiki* and the *Nihon Shoki* are the holy texts of the Shinto religion which pervades Japan to this day. Though we can read these texts as mythology and folklore, they are also read by some as religious texts. The *Kojiki* and the *Nihon Shoki* are the earliest stories which came to form the Shinto religion.

Before delving into the *Kojiki* and the *Nihon Shoki*, it is helpful to survey the basic ideas of the Shinto religion. Shinto is believed to be the indigenous religion and tradition of Japan. As we will see, one of the most critical features of Shinto is ancestor worship, but this is tied to worship of the kami, or, roughly translated, the deities. Since Shinto reveres the natural world as a feature of divine creation, we find kami in every aspect of life and nature. At one time, kami were venerated and worshiped just about anywhere and everywhere. Now one will find jinja, or designated temples specifically for worshiping specific kami.

Kami

Since ancient times, Japanese culture has involved tremendous respect and awe for nature and all features of the natural world. For this reason, just about all aspects of nature are associated with specific kami. So, there is the sun, the moon, and the earth, and there are kami which correspond to each of these. As we will see in the central books which form the basis of Shinto beliefs and practices, there are kami for every aspect of life and death. Those who attend death are ugly and terrifying. But this should not lead us to believe that the kami associated with life are completely benign. Shinto religion accepts that nature is capricious and dangerous. What gives us life is the very thing which takes it away. Kami do not exist simply to please humanity and make life peaceful and easy. The kami of the Shinto religion animates all aspects of life and are therefore an essential feature of things which are unpleasant. The Shinto religion seems to accept that one must take the bitter with the sweet.

Jinja

Throughout the *Kijiki*, for example, we find points in the stories which designate specific geographical locations as the sites where the deities performed certain functions. The gateway to the underworld exists as a real geographic site. Elsewhere, the forms of the kami designate areas for worship and for performing rituals. At one-time, evergreen trees, for example, were decorated to worship and revere kami of nature, and for performing sacred rituals. Over time these areas have been marked by shrines called Jinja. These are primarily temples dedicated to specific kami. They are the familiar pavilion-style structures so closely associated with Japanese culture.

Beyond these ancient texts which remain significant as religious texts to this day, Japanese culture offers a wealth of other mythological stories. The yokai are Japan's fairies and elves. These creatures are difficult to pin down because they are just as inconsistent in their habits and ways as the fairies and elves from other parts of the world.

Yokai can often be extremely dangerous and the three we will look at are the most dangerous. Yokai can be transformed into oni, or demons, at which point they become malevolent and destructive. Other Yokai are merely indifferent creatures who inhabit a space which seems to be just adjacent to our world. They come and go without causing much of a problem unless they perceive a wrong on the part of the human world. As we will see, as much as Japan keeps the lore of the evilest yokai, there is also those Yokai who grant wishes as well.

In addition to these mythological realms, Japan also has its store of fairy tales. The fairy tales of Japan follow themes which are at once familiar and strange. The figure of the dragon looms large in Japanese fairy tales and dragons are not necessarily the fearsome creatures we know from western traditions. Dragons hold a different place in Japanese lore. They are at times quite gentle; other times they hold the position of the highest royalty.

As with the fairy tales we are accustomed to, the Japanese tradition includes tales of simple wonder and magic, and tales designed to teach lessons to children. We will look at just couple of these stories.

Finally, we will look at a hero and heroine from the Japanese mythological tradition. England has it King Arthur, the Greeks had Achilles, and the Romans had Ulysses. The Japanese tradition has characters which serve similar cultural functions. As with the other aspects of Japanese mythology, there are differences from the western myths we may be more accustomed to. But the heroes we will look at are just as brave and majestic in ways which serve the Japanese ideals of heroism.

Chapter 1 – Introduction to the *Kojiki*

One of the most important texts in the mythology of Japan, indeed, possibly the central text for Japanese spiritual culture is the *Kojiki* or *The Record of Ancient Matters*. First compiled in the 8th Century (711-712 CE), the *Kojiki* is the text of the ancient Shinto religion and the spiritual beliefs which underpin it. The creation myths, the stories which have shaped mythology in Japan originate in the *Kojiki*. The origins of the Emperors is found in this text. The Emperors of Japan found their roots in the Gods who gave rise to the islands of Japan.

There are three main sections to the *Kojiki*. The first is the *Kamitsumaki*. This contains the preface to the *Kojiki* and the stories of the Age of the Gods. It also includes the creation stories—the creation and founding of Japan and the origin of the Emperors. The second section, the *Nakatsumaki*, begins with the story of the first Emperor, Jimmu. This recounts his conquest of Japan and takes the reader up to the 15th Emperor, Ojin. Finally, the text traces the reigns of the 16th through 33rd Emperors in what is titled *Shimotsumaki*. The third and final section shows limited interaction between the human world and the gods.

The *Kojiki* mixes the realms of human and divine in a manner we recognize from other mythological systems. The Judeo-Christian bible offers numerous tales of these interactions between humans and God. The Greeks and Romans built their entire modes of belief and their entire myth structure out of the dialogue between Gods and humans. The *Kojiki* follows a similar pattern with the gods receding from intimate contact with the human realm the closer we get to recorded history.

The *Kojiki*, like most other great texts of ancient origins, has a clouded history. Most scholars agree that much of the text is cribbed from Chinese mythology to the extent that China exerted a tremendous influence on early Japanese culture. Until roughly the 8th Century, most of the myths and legends of Japan were kept privately by individual families. It was the Emperor Temmu in 681 who became adamant on compiling these myths and legends into one text. It laid dormant for twenty-five years before finally being completed. No matter the various sources, the central place of the *Kojiki* to modern Japanese culture and modern Shinto practice cannot be denied. The *Kojiki* stands as a Japanese text.

The Creation Stories

Like nearly all mythological systems, the *Kojiki* begins with the creation myths. The text begins with the creation of seven deities. Most agree that the crux of the creation myth begins with the brother and sister gods, Izanagi and Izanami, who set in motion the birth of the lands and the peoples who would come. We are told this brother and sister are granted a heavenly jeweled spear which they dip into the briny water. When they pull the spear up, it drips the brine onto the oil which was the primal space before the creation of the earth until an island was formed: "This is the Island of Onogoro," as the text explains.

From here the *Kojiki* relates the creation of natural forces such as the sun, the moon, and fire all who are enlivened by attendant gods and goddesses. Most notable of these are the Sun Goddess and her brother, Susano-o, and the conflicts between the two of them. Susano-o is seen as the rebel in the text, analogous to other rebels in mythology such as Loki in the Norse tradition. He is also referred to as being evil which would make him something like the devil except that Japanese tradition consists of other demon characters. It is from Susano-o that the Emperors dynasties are traced.

The next two sections are more generally concerned with the vast genealogies of royal lines. Beginning with the supernatural beings and tales, the *Kojiki* recounts the rise of the mythological Emperor and Empress Jimmu and Sojin. We read of the rise of the mythological heroes Yamato-Take and Jin-go. In all, the text traces the genealogies of 17 Emperors over many centuries.

There is an entire literature of scholarship on the *Kojiki,* and you could spend your life studying this text. The importance of this book cannot be stressed enough since it is one of the founding texts of both the Shinto religion and the origin of Japanese national identity.

For the western reader, it is easy to get confused while reading the *Kojiki*. The names are unfamiliar, and some of the features of the mythology are unknown to us. There is a strange significance to the number eight, whereas in the Judeo-Christian tradition it is the number seven. The tremendous importance Izanami places on her shame may be foreign to some readers. However, there are numerous points of reference which will be quite familiar. The mysterious beginnings of the deities are strikingly similar to the unfathomable origins of gods in other myths. The tension between the heavens, the earth, and the underworld are all familiar to us. And the tricky intelligence of the hero, Susano-o, should come as no surprise.

Since the *Kojiki* contains such a vast amount of information, including long genealogies of Emperors, it is helpful to focus on a few of the mythologies included in the text. Of interest is the ancient Japanese story of Creation and Origins and the rise of Susano-o, the great hero, and trickster of the *Kojiki*.

The Myths of Origins

Before Creation, the Center of Heaven Deity and The Reproducing Deity existed in the Plain of High Heaven. Next Came the Wondrous Reproducing Deity. These Deities lived alone when all creation consisted of the Earth and the Sea. The Earth and the Sea were unformed and existed as an oil. The *Kojiki* explains that the Earth and Sea floated medusa-like over the oil. Next came the Pleasant-Reed-Shoot-Prince-Elder-Deity and the Heavenly-Eternally-Standing-Deity. This leads to the time of The Seven Divine Generations which first are the Earthly-Eternally-Standing-Deity and the Luxuriant-Integrating-Master-Deity. What follows are the Mud-Earth-Lord and his sister Mud-Earth-Lady. Next appear the Germ-Earth-Integrating –Deity and his sister Life-Integrating-Deity. Finally, the order of the original Deities are as follows: Elder-of-the-Great-Place and his sister Elder-Lady-of-the-Great-Place; Perfect-Exterior and his sister Oh-Awful-Lady; Male-Who-Invites and his sister Female-Who-Invites. These are the generations of the Deities who precede the creation of the world.

With all the Deities assembled it is commanded that Male-Who-Invites, Izanagi, and his sister Female-Who-Invites, Izanami, are to give birth to a drifting island. These are the two principle created deities. They are given a jeweled spear. The two deities stand on the Floating Bridge of Heaven and plunge the jeweled spear into the brine of the unformed sea. Upon withdrawing the spear, the brine drips down and forms the island of Onogoro which means "self-condensed." This is the origin of the first creation. The islands which would come to make up Japan are derived from this moment in the *Kojiki*.

The Journey to the Underworld

After the creation of the islands and the things in the world, Izanami gave birth to the fire god, Kagutsuchi. In the process, she was burned terribly and eventually died from her injuries. Izanagi buried her on Mt. Hiba and her spirit descended to Yomi-no-kuni which is the underworld.

After Izanami was gone, Izanagi missed her and decided to go find her. He traveled to Mt. Hiba and found the gates of Yomi-no-kuni. Izanami's spirit greeted him at the gates. Izanagi told her they were not finished with the creation of the world. He wanted her to come back with him, but she told him she had already eaten of the food of the earth and could no longer leave. She contemplates her brother's visit and words and says that since he has traveled all this way she could talk to the lord of this world. She explains that Izanagi must wait. She explicitly tells him that he must not look at her.

After some time has passed, Izanagi became impatient. Breaking a tooth off the comb he had in his hair, he made a torch to light his way and pursued her. He entered Yomi-no-kuni and found her rotting. She was crawling with maggots. Eight gods of thunder hung from her body. Izanagi was terrified and fled. Izanami told him: "I told you not to look at me. You have caused me great shame." With this, she ordered the evil hags of the underworld to chase him.

Izanagi ran, but the hags started to catch up to him. In desperation, he threw a band from his hair onto the ground which changed into a grapevine full of grapes. This slowed the hags as they paused to eat the grapes, but they ate faster than Izanagi had hoped, and they quickly caught up with him. This time, he broke another tooth from his comb and threw it on the ground where bamboo shoots sprung forth. The hags paused to eat the bamboo shoots and again they were slowed in their pursuit of Izanagi.

Izanami, seeing that Izanagi would escape, ordered the gods of thunder and an army of evil spirits to chase him. Izanagi pulled out his sword and swung at his attackers but to no avail. He ran on. As he approached the gates of the underworld, he came upon a peach tree. Plucking three peaches, he hurled them at his attackers and drove them back into the underworld.

This time, Izanami herself went after him. Izanagi took a giant boulder and blocked the entrance to Yomi-no-kuni, forever separating the underworld from the earth and himself from Izanami. Here they said their final farewells.

Izanami pronounced a curse: Everyday she would kill one thousand people from the world for the shame Izanagi has caused her. Izanagi replied that in return, he would 'people the earth' with five thousand inhabitants. They never saw each other again.

Izanagi bathed himself to remove the filth of the underworld. In doing this, many new deities were born. Of these, the sun goddess, Amaterasu, came forth as Izanagi washed his left eye. From his right eye, Tsukuyomi, the deity of the moon was born.

Izanagi loved his children and gave them each a realm. Amaterasu was given the heavens. To Tsukuyomi, he gave the night. A third deity, Susano-o, who came into being as Izanagi washed his nose, was given the seas.

These new deities were happy with their realms. However, Susano-o was rebellious. He acted out against Izanagi. For this, he was banished to the Earth.

The Wanderings of Susano-o

After he was banished to earth, Susano-o found himself wandering up the river Hii to the land of Izumo. He noticed some chopsticks floating down the river and decided to see who may have lost them. He finally came upon an elderly couple and their daughter, Kushinada-hime. The couple were crying in despair, and Susano-o asked them why. They explained that their daughter was to be sacrificed to the serpent monster, Yamata-no-Orochi. This monster was foul, with eight heads and eight tails; its body long enough to cover eight mountain peaks. It was covered with moss and trees, and its underside was inflamed and smeared with blood.

Susano-o further discovered that the couple initially had eight daughters, all of whom had been sacrificed to Yamata-no-Orochi each year until they were only left with Kushinada-hime. Susano-o told the couple that if they gave him their daughter's hand in marriage, he would slay the serpent. To which they happily agreed.

Susano-o set about his preparations. He first turned Yamata-no-Orochi into a comb and placed her in his hair. Next, he instructed the couple to brew some strong sake. They were to build a fence around the house with eight gates. He then instructed them to build a platform and place a vat filled with the sake inside each gate. After the preparations were complete, he told them to wait.

Susano-o knew that serpents loved sake, and as he expected, each of the serpent's eight heads dipped into all eight vats of sake and drank until the serpent was quite drunk. It soon passed out from being drunk.

Susano-o watched from his safe hiding place. As soon as he saw the Yamata-no-Orochii was drunk and passed out, he sprang from his spot and cut the serpent to pieces until the river Hii ran red with its blood.

As Susano-o was cutting the serpent's tail, he struck something which broke his blade. As he examined the cut, he discovered a sword. He quickly realized this was no ordinary sword. Seeing its importance, Susano-o offered the sword to his sister, Amaterasu, the deity of the sun and ruler of the heavens. The sword was called Kusunagi-no-tsurugi, or the Great Sword of Kusunagi. This became one of the three great Imperial Treasures of Japan.

Having slain the hideous serpent Yamata-no-Orichi, and finding Kushinada-himi safe, Susano-o began searching for a place suitable to build a palace. After a time, he arrived in Suga. Here he decided this was the place where he felt at peace, and he built his palace. Soon after, a large cloud appeared. Susano-o looked up at the sky and recited his poem:

Izumo is a land protected by clouds aplenty

And like this land of Izumo

I shall build a fence to protect the palace

Where my wife will live

Like the clouds in the land of Izumo

With this, Susano-o appointed his father-in-law, Ashinazuchi, to be caretaker of the place. Susano-o and Kushinada-himi lived in the palace at Suga. It is believed that the poem Susano-o recited is the origin of traditional Japanese poetry such as waka and haiku.

Chapter 2 – Introduction to the *Nihon Shoki*

In addition to the *Kojiki,* the other central text in Japanese religion and spirituality is the *Nihon Shoki.* This text contains many of the same tales concerning the origins of the world and the gods, but it provides some alternative stories that offer more details on the lives and adventures of the gods and early heroes and heroines.

The primary significance of the *Nihon Shoki* is the lengthy genealogies which provide the origins of royal dynasties and the divine origins of the Emperors. Whereas this information occupies mainly the last two-thirds of the *Kojiki*, the details of critical genealogical lines would appear to be the primary focus and purpose of the *Nihom Shoki.* Nevertheless, this text does contain a wealth of mythological material.

In the *Nihon Shoki,* we encounter the same mythological figures. Izanami and Izanagi are present, and their importance to the birth of Japan are identical. Some of the other characters are slightly different. The birth of the sun, moon, and various features of the earth are detailed in the *Nihon Shoki,* and we will explore some of these stories. We will encounter the hero and troublemaker Susano-o, only in this text, he appears as Susawono. It is the same trickster figure from the *Kojiki.*

The Birth of Amaterasu, Trukuyumi, Susawono, and the Leech-Child

Each of these tales is broken into various versions. Apparently, the oral tradition from which this text was compiled, pulled together a wide variety of source material. One may conjecture that the earliest scribes of the *Nihon Shoki* deemed all versions of the tale to be worthy of preservation and study. For this reason, they preserved and transcribed the repetition we find in the collection of stories. The following summary is from Section Five, Main Version.

After they have made way for the creation of the Earth and the islands of Japan, Izanami and Izanagi made the sea, the rivers, and the mountains. They gave birth to Kukunochi, the ancestor of the trees and Kusanohime, the ancestor of the grass, who is also called Notsuchi.

Izanami and Izanagi spoke to each other and said: "We have already given birth to the eight-island country, its rivers, its trees, and its grasses; why don't we give birth to rulers of this country." At which they gave birth to Ohirume no Muchi who is also called Amaterasu. This is the sun goddess. The child was so bright that she shined on every quarter of Japan. Izanami and Izanagi rejoiced at their daughter, and they said "Though our breaths have been many, we have yet to make one to equal this child. She should not reside in this country. She should be sent to heaven, and she should be given heavenly duties." Using the pillar of the earth, they sent her to heaven.

After this, they gave birth to the moon god who is called Tsukuyomi no Mikoto. He shone brightly like his sister and was sent to heaven.

They then gave birth to the leech-child. Even as he reached the age of three, his legs would not allow him to stand. He was placed in a boat of hardened camphor and cast to the winds.

The next born was Susawono no Mikoto. In another version, he is called Kamususanowo no Mikoto. Susawono no Mikoto was brazen and committed many acts of disrespect. He also had a habit of frequently weeping and wailing. He caused many people in the country to die. He once caused two green mountains to wither. For this, Izanami and Izanagi banished him from their realm. He was sent to distant Nenokuni.

The Story of the Comb and the Curse

The story of Izanami and Izanagi in which she is transformed into an ugly demon and the subsequent journey into the underworld is re-told in *Nihon Shoki* with some differences. It is worth presenting this alternative version since this tale is central to the mythological Traditions of Japan.

Izanagi followed Izanami to the land of Yomi. When they spoke, Izanami told him "Why have you come so late? I have already eaten the food of this world. I must rest so; please do not look at me." Izanagi would not listen. He took his comb out of his hair and broke off a tooth. With this, he made a torch. When he looked at her, she was horrifying. Pus spurted from her and maggots crawled on her. For this reason, people to this day hate to carry a single torch at night and refuse to throw a comb on the ground.

Izanagi exclaimed "I have unknowingly visited a polluted land," and he quickly ran away. Izanami said with shame and remorse "Why didn't you listen to me? Now you have put me to shame." With this, she let loose the eight ugly women of Yomi to pursue him and trap him in Yomi.

Izanagi pulled out his sword. Swinging it behind him as he fled. He threw away his black headpiece, and it was transformed into grapes. The eight ugly women stopped to eat the grapes. When they were finished, the continued to pursue him. Izanagi then threw down his comb, and it was transformed into bamboo shoots. Again, the eight ugly women stopped to eat the bamboo shoots and then quickly pursued him. Finally, Inzanagi pursued Izanami herself, but at this time he was already at the border of Yomi and the living word.

At the border of Yomi, Izanagi lifted a giant boulder just as the women were approaching him. Izanagi took the rock and blocked the exit from Yomi. He pronounced the oath of divorce from Izanami.

Izanagi told him "If you say this oath I will strangle 1,000 people from this world every day you are a ruler." In response, Izanagi said "If you do such a thing I will cause 1,500 children to be born every day. Do not come beyond this point. He threw down his staff, called Funato no Kami; then he threw down his belt, called Nagachiha no Kami; then he threw down his robe called Wazurahi no Kami; then he threw down his pants, which are called Akikuhi no Kami; then he threw down his shoes, called Chishiki no Kami. The boulder remains to block the passage to the underworld.

[The passage to the underworld may not actually be a physical space, but rather, a state or period between when you stop breathing and when you actually die].

Continue reading

Check out this book

Preview of Greek Mythology

Captivating Greek Myths of Greek Gods, Goddesses, Monsters and Heroes

Introduction

Giants. Gods. Heroes. Monsters. These are the stuff of Greek myths and legends. These ancient stories tell the tales of the before-time, when the heavens and the earth were new, and when great deeds were done by beings who were larger than life.

The ancient Greeks had no concept of a unitary creator-god or set of creator-gods. For the ancient Greeks, the world simply came into being out of Nothingness. But for the Greeks, that Nothingness was in itself a being: the name of the first primordial god, Chaos, in fact, means "Chasm" or "Abyss," and into this abyss Mother Earth also came into being, unmade and unassisted. Greek creation myths also differ from those of for example the book of Genesis in that it's not only plants and animals that come into being through the actions of the gods. Things like Night, Death, Sleep, and Memory also were considered sentient beings that had their places in the ladder of creation and that deserved respect—if not worship—of mortal humans.

In addition to explaining how creation itself began, myths in many cultures have the function of "just-so" stories, explaining various other important things—the invention of fire, why we have weather, the names of plants and birds. Greek mythology is no different: enfolded in grand stories of gods and heroes are some of the ways the ancient Greeks understood many of the more common aspects of their world.

The world was a dangerous place for the ancient Greeks. Disease and famine, war and death were always around the corner and waiting to strike when one least expected it. The ancient Greeks thought that misfortune was the result of the caprice of the gods. Therefore, these myths also function as cautionary tales, warning humans of the sin of hubris, telling them to be humble and worship the gods as was just and right, so that maybe the gods would smile and take pity on the mortals they ruled.

Although the gods and goddesses were powerful immortal beings, they were in many ways still very like the humans who worshiped them and who created these tales. The gods and goddesses are stricken with jealousy; they fall in love; they get angry when they feel slighted, and bestow gifts when they are honored. Likewise, the heroes are larger than life: they're stronger, faster, and more skilled than ordinary mortals, but they are still subject to pain, illness, and death.

There are usually several different versions of these myths, which were told and retold over a span of many centuries. The versions presented here are an amalgamation from various ancient Greek sources. My goal has not been to create an "official" text, so sometimes I have mingled variants from different sources to create a single compelling narrative that at the same time is faithful to ancient ways of remembering these stories, which still have so much to tell us even today.

Part I

The Golden Age of the Titans

The Creation of the Titans

In the beginning, there was only Chaos. Out of Chaos came Darkness and Night. Night was mother to both Air and Day, but also to Doom, Death, Sleep, and Old Age, and many other children besides, and Darkness was their father.

After Chaos came Gaia, who is Mother Earth, and then Eros, the god of love. Gaia herself brought forth Uranus, that is Father Sky, and with him, Gaia made the first and oldest gods, the Titans, who governed the universe and peopled it with their divine children. Some of these children were fair beings, who themselves gave birth to gods and goddesses, but others were fearsome to behold. These were the Cyclops, great giants with only one eye each, and the Hecatoncheires, the Hundred-Handed Ones, three brothers with fifty heads and one hundred arms each. Father Sky feared the Cyclops and the Hecatoncheires. He captured them and imprisoned them in Tartarus, a terrible, dark cavern deep under the earth, from which nothing could escape.

Besides the Cyclops and Hundred-Handed Ones, together Mother Earth and Father Sky had twelve children, six males, who were Oceanus, Hyperion, Coeus, Cronus, Crius, and Iapetus; and six females, Mnemosyne (Memory), Tethys, Theia, Phoebe, Rhea, and Themis.

Uranus was jealous of his children and hid them away in a cavern deep inside Gaia. As Uranus put each child inside their mother, Gaia began to feel the pain of over-fullness, so she went and created a great sickle of adamant, the hardest of all metals, and showed it to her children.

"Which of you will take this sickle, and free us from Father Sky's oppression?" said Mother Earth.

But Gaia's children were all terrified of their father, and none would step forward to take the sickle, until one day Cronus said, "Give me the sickle, Mother. I will do as you ask."

Gaia hid Cronus away where Uranus would not see him and told him what he should do. As the day ended, Father Sky came to Mother Earth, covering her with night and wanting to make love to her. And when Uranus was stretched out over the fair Earth, Cronus took the sickle of adamant and cut his father's genitals off. Cronus cast these away behind him. Drops of Uranus' blood landed on Gaia and were taken into her, and from these were made the Furies, Alecto, Tisiphone, and Magaera, the goddesses of vengeance; and the Giants; and the nymphs of the trees.

Uranus' genitals landed in the ocean. As they floated on the water, white foam began to grow around them. The white foam grew and took the shape of a young woman, the purest and most beautiful of all. She stepped out of the water onto the island of Cyprus and is called Aphrodite, the goddess of love. Aphrodite had two helpers at her birth: Eros, the god of love, and Himeros, god of desire, who was born with her.

Once the Titans were all freed from the cavern, they took one another as husbands and wives and began to make children of their own. The Sun, Moon, and the Dawn were all children of Hyperion and Theia. Oceanus, the great sea that encircles the whole world, and his wife Tethys, were the parents of many mighty rivers, including the Nile and the Danube, and of Metis, the first wife of Zeus and mother of Athena, goddess of wisdom. Atlas, who holds the sky on his shoulders, and Prometheus, bringer of fire, and ill-fated Epimetheus were the sons of Iapetus and Asia, who herself was an Oceanid, a daughter of Oceanus and Tethys. Many of these Titans and children of Titans have stories of their own, some of which will be told later.

The Birth of the Olympians and the Downfall of the Titans

By far the most important descendants of the Titans were the Olympians, children of Rhea and Cronus, who eventually overthrew the older gods and came to rule over all creation from the heights of Mount Olympus, with Father Zeus at their head. And this is how that came to pass.

Rhea and Cronus, Titans both and children of Mother Earth and Father Sky, lived as husband and wife, and Rhea bore Cronus many children. But Cronus was jealous and grasping and had heard his reign over all that was would be ended by one of his children. Every time Rhea bore him a child, Cronus snatched it away and ate it, first Hestia, then Demeter, Hera, Hades, and Poseidon, one after the other, thinking that would protect him and secure his throne forever.

This made Rhea deeply sorrowful, so the next time she felt herself with child, she begged her parents, Mother Earth and Father Sky, for help. They agreed to help her, guiding her to a cave on the island of Crete, where Zeus was born and where Rhea hid her son far, far away within Gaia. There Zeus lived, cared for by his grandmother until he was grown.

After Rhea left Zeus in the cave, she swaddled a rock to make it look like a baby, and brought it to Cronus, saying, "See, here is your new-born son."

Cronus was so hasty in his jealousy and fear he swallowed the rock whole, without even looking at it. Then he was satisfied, thinking that he could never be overthrown since he had imprisoned every one of his children inside himself.

Meanwhile, in the cave on the island of Crete, Zeus grew in stature and might, and when he deemed the time was right, he left the cave and went searching for his father. He found mighty Cronus, and they had a fierce battle. Zeus was too strong for wicked Cronus and forced him to vomit up all his brothers and sisters. The first thing Cronus vomited up was the rock he had swallowed in Zeus' place. Then out came Poseidon, Hades, Hera, Demeter, and Hestia, one after the other. The rock Zeus kept, as a memorial to his victory, and had it placed in Pytho, on holy Mount Parnassus.

It became clear to Zeus that something needed to be done about who wielded power in the universe. Was it to be the old gods, the Titans? Or was it to be the younger gods and goddesses, the Olympians, who were his brothers and sisters? Clearly the Titans were not to be trusted: Zeus' father had eaten his children, after all, and Zeus had escaped that fate himself only through the courage and resourcefulness of his mother. Zeus knew he was strong, and so were his brothers and sisters, but he also knew he would need help. The first ones he decided to call upon were the Cyclops, terrible, one-eyed giants named Brontes (Thunderer), Steropes (Lightning), and Arges (Brightness), all of whom were gifted makers and smiths.

Now, the Cyclops had been imprisoned in Tartarus, a terrible, dark cavern far below the earth, from which there was no escape. Uranus, Father Sky, had placed them there for the first time, long ago, and there they stayed, until Cronus, father of the Olympian gods, freed them and asked them to help him overthrow Uranus. The Cyclops helped Cronus with a good will, and Uranus was overthrown, but wicked Cronus double-crossed the Cyclops: as soon as they were no longer of any use to him, he imprisoned them in Tartarus once again.

Zeus braved the terrible deeps of Tartarus and freed the Cyclops from their prison. In thanks for their freedom, they made thunder and lightning and gave these to Zeus, which he could then use in his battles with the Titans or whenever else he might have need of them. The Cyclops also bestowed a trident upon Poseidon and gave a helmet to Hades.

The Cyclops were not the only ones who Zeus freed from Tartarus. The Hecatoncheires, the Hundred-Handed Ones, Cottus (Furious), Briareus (Vigorous), and Gyges (Big-Limbed) were three sons of Uranus, and their mother was Gaia. These brothers each had fifty heads and a hundred arms and were fearsomely strong and brave in battle. These three brothers also had been imprisoned in Tartarus by Father Sky, and it was Rhea, mother of Zeus, who gave her son the idea to free these three brothers also, saying that if Zeus released them, he could call upon them for help when he needed it. Zeus followed his mother's advice. He descended again into the pit of Tartarus and freed the Hundred-Handed Ones who, as Rhea had said, then promised to fight for Zeus whenever he called.

With the weapons of the Cyclops and the help of the Hundred-Handed Ones, Zeus and the Olympians went to war against the Titans. There was a mighty battle, and in the end, the Titans were defeated. Zeus then imprisoned them in Tartarus and set the Hundred-Handed Ones to guard them. The next thing to be done was to divide up the rule of the universe. Zeus, the god of thunder and lightning, took the sky. Poseidon, the god of the sea, took the oceans and seas, and Hades was allotted the Underworld, the place of the Dead which also bears his name.

Continue Reading

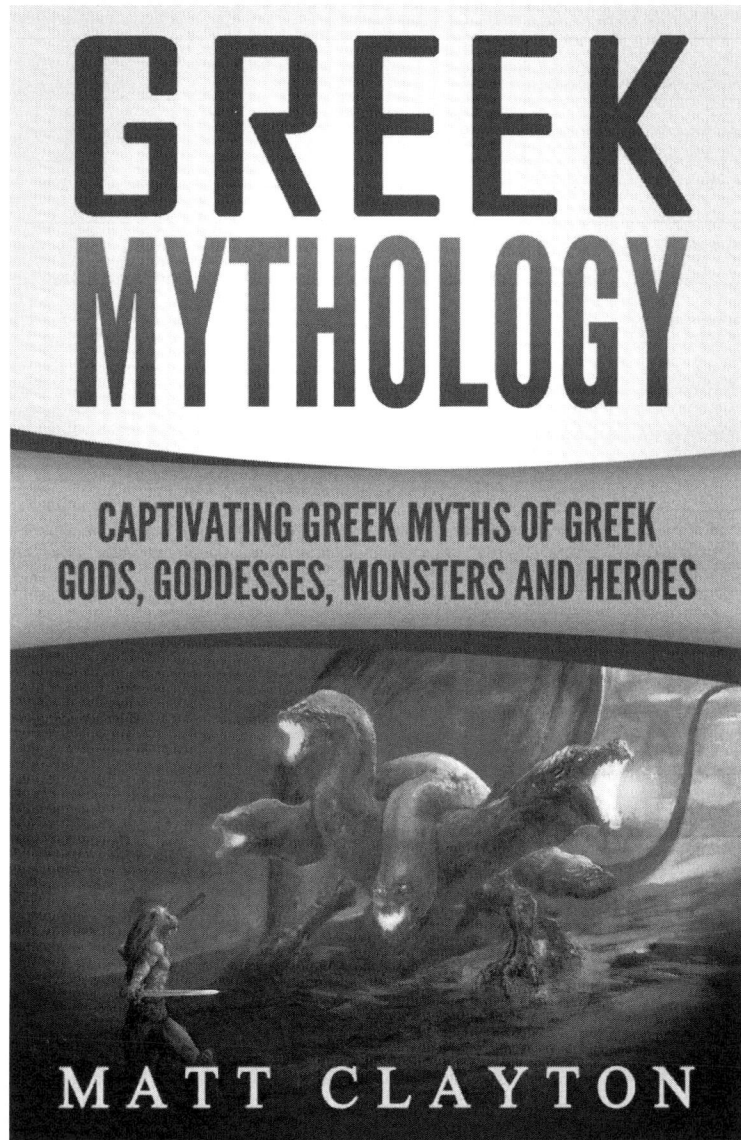

GREEK MYTHOLOGY

CAPTIVATING GREEK MYTHS OF GREEK GODS, GODDESSES, MONSTERS AND HEROES

MATT CLAYTON

Check out this book

Bibliography

Birrel, Anne (1999), Chinese Mythology: An Introduction.

Chew, Katherine Liang (2002), Tales of the Teahouse Retold: Investiture of the Gods.

Walters, Derek (1995), An Encyclopedia of Myth and Legend: Chinese Mythology.

Wilkinson, Philip (2011), Myths and Legends.

Yang, Lihui and An Deming, with Jessica Anderson Turner (2005), Handbook of Chinese Mythology.

Websites:

Worldstories.org.uk

www.shenyunperformingarts.org

https://en.wikisource.org/wiki/Portal:Investiture_of_the_Gods/

Free Bonus from Captivating History (Available for a Limited time)

Hi History Lovers!

Now you have a chance to join our exclusive history list so you can get your first history ebook for free as well as discounts and a potential to get more history books for free! Simply visit the link below to join.

Captivatinghistory.com/ebook

Also, make sure to follow us on:

Twitter: @Captivhistory

Facebook: Captivating History:@captivatinghistory

Printed in Great Britain
by Amazon